Praise
Conversations with the Z's, Book One

"Lee Harris is one of the clearest and most potent channels of our time."

— **Kyle Gray**, bestselling author of
Raise Your Vibration and *Angel Numbers*

"While I've enjoyed collaborating with many spiritual teachers and healers during my time as a past-life psychic over the past two decades, every now and then I meet one with an extra-special gift. Lee Harris is among the very best. Not only is he an enlightened old soul, he's also a kind and compassionate human whose work is helping elevate our collective consciousness. Lee's new book is everything he is — insightful, engaging, and filled with wisdom."

— **Ainslie MacLeod**, past-life psychic, spiritual teacher, and author of *The Instruction*

"Deep, humorous, moving, educational, and mind-blowing cosmic conversation between a down-to-earth psychotherapist and the chatty guides of channeler Lee Harris. All you need is an open mind and heart to begin. Highly recommended to anyone searching for spiritual solace in these chaotic times. Expect to be amazed."

— **Colette Baron-Reid**, oracle expert, spiritual intuitive, and bestselling author of *The Spirit Animal Oracle*

"Lee Harris is a uniquely gifted human, a purehearted spiritual channel bringing through the healing wisdom needed to awaken our world."

— **Alana Fairchild**, musician and
bestselling author of *Sacred Rebels Oracle*

"Lee Harris is as open and heart-centered a channel as you'll encounter. And his guides, the Z's, are clear, poignant, and joyful messengers of grounding insight and wisdom. At a time when our reality can feel more disconnected and overwhelming than ever, these conversations reconnected me to the soulful truths of our humanity and divinity, and encouraged me to trust more deeply in life's unfolding. Lee and the Z's help me feel more at peace and at home here, and that in itself is a miracle."

— **Scott Stabile**, author of *Big Love:
The Power of Living with a Wide-Open Heart*

CONVERSATIONS

WITH THE

Z's

BOOK ONE

ALSO BY LEE HARRIS

Energy Speaks:
Messages from Spirit on Living, Loving, and Awakening

CONVERSATIONS

WITH THE

Z's

BOOK ONE

The Energetics of the New Human Soul

LEE HARRIS

with DIANNA EDWARDS

New World Library
Novato, California

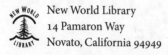 New World Library
14 Pamaron Way
Novato, California 94949

Text design by Tona Pearce Myers

Library of Congress Cataloging-in-Publication data is available.

First printing, September 2022
ISBN 978-1-60868-838-8
Ebook ISBN 978-1-60868-839-5
Printed in Canada on 100% postconsumer-waste recycled paper

 New World Library is proud to be a Gold Certified Environmentally Responsible Publisher. Publisher certification awarded by Green Press Initiative.

10   9   8   7   6   5   4   3   2

CONTENTS

A NOTE FROM LEE

Conversations can be powerful and multidimensional. They have the capacity to guide us, educate us, soothe us, entertain us, and in more ways than we often realize, they help us to become who we are.

I had never really considered that until this week, as I was preparing to write the opening words for this book, and this awareness came to me very strongly. We often give full credit to the times when we go within, get silent or still, meditate — but we forget how influenced we are by the everyday act of conversation that we may participate in or listen to.

I realized that it has most often been through dialogue with others that I have broadened my perspective and learned something new about the person I am speaking with or, indeed, about myself.

I still remember powerful words of wisdom delivered through conversation with my grandmother some twenty years ago, or something my dad said to me when I was a teenager that changed and expanded the way I saw the world. Neither of these two loves of my life are still with us on the physical, but their words shaped who I have become, and I have no doubt that they will remain a part of my memories forever.

While these types of Earthly dialogues have been profoundly helpful to me, I've also been blessed to participate in a series of conversations that have been even more influential in terms of my understanding spirituality, life's larger questions, and the energy of our world. I have been having life-changing channeled dialogue with my guides, the Z's, for exactly half my life now. I first heard them when I was twenty-three years old.

It was a total surprise as it was not something I was seeking. It was also surprising because our first meeting happened in one of the most unlikely places. I was traveling on a London Underground train when the Z's, a group of beings from the ninth dimension, clearly and coherently introduced themselves to me.

I was sitting on the subway sifting through the usual judgmental thoughts in my head, thoughts mostly focused on judging myself and aspects of my life that I was unhappy about. Today, we often hear this referred to as "negative self-talk," but back then I just knew it as "normal."

But that day, as I rode to work and mentally reviewed a situation I felt unhappy about, I heard a voice tell me, "That's an interesting thought, but you're wrong."

My hearing this other voice marked a paradigm shift. Unbeknownst to me, this day was to be the day that the lights went on in my life and awareness. And it began a relationship with my guides that would forever change, influence, and expand me.

From the first moment I heard their words, the difference in their clarity, certainty, and energetic brightness versus my own negative self-talk was palpable. The wisdom and love in their advice and the physically uplifting energy I felt, and have felt every time I've connected with them since, is profound and undeniable.

People often ask if I was afraid when I first heard my guides. I always give the same answer to that question: not at all — they felt like home. I was, however, immediately concerned with how others might perceive me because of this experience I was having.

My first channeled book, *Energy Speaks*, shares in detail the full story of how I first met them and the changes and learning I went through as a result. The book then goes on to present a broad range of topics and teachings from the Z's, created from the first decade of "lectures" that they had delivered live through me during public workshops and audio recordings.

This new book was a surprise to me, as it wasn't exactly "planned," but then where the Z's are concerned, I have learned to surrender to that magic over time. I am delighted to be presenting a new chapter with the Z's and one that takes us in a fresh direction: into the art of a conversation with them.

Facilitated by my good friend Dianna Edwards, these conversations reveal and allow a whole other way of understanding their perspectives on the world we live in and the times we are going through. They also offer new insight into who the Z's are, how they see the world, and why they are connected to us.

I can't think of a better dialogue partner for them than Dianna. She is not only a very gifted psychotherapist but also a spiritual "old soul" who is deeply connected to her own wisdom and intuition.

We became friends years ago when she came to me for a private session, back when I was still offering them. She explained that it was not her norm to go for sessions like this as she was very discerning about working with other practitioners, but that something made her want to connect with me and the Z's. Now, several years of friendship later, we laugh at how we were brought together and what has transpired. With the advent of these books, we can both now also see the bigger reason why we were brought together.

We have supported each other through our friendship, and during that time, we've had many different private conversations with the Z's about all kinds of matters. The potency of those conversations and Dianna's gift with questions made me ask Dianna to do some recordings with me for my members' community, The Portal. We originally thought it would be just a few facilitated conversations, but as soon as we began conversation one, it became clear that these conversations had a larger arc and a greater purpose beyond the starting point we had both agreed to.

The Z's wanted these books to happen and told me so the night of the first recorded conversation. They have given us a blueprint for a whole series of conversations, to be transcribed and published as books, and here is where it begins. Dianna and I are delighted we have joined forces to do this, and I am grateful to her for being willing.

It may seem like my biggest job as a channeler is allowing the words and energy to flow through me, and that is true when I am in the moment of channeling. But it is also true that, as Lee, my biggest learning comes through when I actually listen to what has been channeled through me. Hearing what my guides had to say, later on as a listener or reader, and noticing when my body feels, heals, or rises in response to the truths they are sharing, is how I get to notice my own expansion from this material, just as I know many of you will experience yours too.

I hope you enjoy these conversations and they uplift, inform, expand, and entertain you. Perhaps more than anything, I hope they help you to remember your brilliance, your light, and your unique purpose at this time on Earth. That is what the Z's continually remind us of.

For we are all needed, and now is our time.

With love,
Lee Harris
February 2022

A NOTE FROM DIANNA

If you were going to have a conversation with a group of eighty-eight ninth-dimensional beings, what would you want to talk about?

That is the question I reviewed for the nearly three months before recording the first of what would be an extensive series of conversations with the Z's.

The Z's are the guides of my friend, Lee Harris. Lee is a well-known channeler, intuitive, and musician. His songs channel frequency and light as much as his words do. The combination of the two is both comforting and life empowering in these unique times on Earth.

For over twenty years, Lee has been sharing the multi-dimensional messages from the Z's, first with private clients and small groups and now with hundreds of thousands each month all over the world.

What do I mean by "multidimensional"? Well, the Z's get to that in these conversations. In fact, it is one of the cornerstones of the conversations.

In one of our private discussions on life and purpose, Lee and I were chatting about what would be most helpful to bring forward to his audience next. I casually mentioned that I would like to interview the Z's extensively about conscious living and dying.

Within minutes of my comment, Lee, whom the Z's have called a "volcano of creativity," was off and running with plans and ideas for a series of conversations with the Z's that would cover a multitude of topics. The Z's were chiming in as well.

The planned conversations offered the Z's a new format in which to create and communicate their messages. Lee, who is one of the fastest architects of creativity I have ever worked with, was already sharing numerous timelines for the work to happen within a few short months.

It was clear that my idea for a conversation about conscious living and dying had lain the groundwork for a much bigger conversation. I asked Lee what we were going to focus on. He immediately heard the title, "The Energetics of the New Human Soul."

I replied, "Sounds good. Shall we make a list of questions and subjects to talk about?"

"Oh, they know you can do that," Lee casually stated as his mind went on to his next project, as creative volcanoes tend to do.

While I appreciated the vote of confidence from both the Z's and Lee, I was left with the question I asked above:

If you were going to have a conversation with a group of eighty-eight ninth-dimensional beings, what would you want to talk about?

I had two and a half months to figure this out. In those months of preparation, I came to the following conclusions:

- There was no guarantee that the conversations would be linear. The Z's speak in spirals and circles, and I would have to track the topics addressed in those spirals and go back and pick up missing pieces in follow-up questions or conversations.
- Yes/no questions were not an option.
- I would need to ask questions that were of interest not just to me but to Lee's audience as a whole. And that audience consisted both of people new to the work of Lee and the Z's and his existing community members, who already were familiar with some of the subject matter.

One of the skills I am seeking to bring to this project is clarity and a focus on the importance of what I call "listening to hear, not listening to respond." Listening to hear has become quite a lost superpower, in my opinion.

If we listen to really hear what is being expressed, not just in the words but in the frequency behind those words, then the next question or response will ring true and deepen the conversation. If we just listen to respond, it tends to bring a shallower quality that carries a lower frequency, which is of benefit to no one.

In these conversations, I was not only listening to hear the Z's as they spoke, but I was listening to hear the wider multi-dimensional audience.

As you journey through the conversations with us, you may notice that the "plot" never resolves; a definitive conclusion is never reached. You may even find that when you reread a conversation a day or month later, it feels different to you. That is due to the dimensional energetics you are access-ing at the time you read this book. The closest metaphor to explain the rather unexplainable energy of that dynamic is seeing the conversations as spirals of information that often have their own spirals of information. Intrigued? I will let the Z's explain the rest.

Welcome to *Conversations with the Z's.* I hope you find them as inspiring as I do.

Dianna Edwards
February 2022

ABOUT THE CONVERSATIONS

These conversations between Dianna and the Z's took place privately in November 2021 and were recorded in audio form.

The text for this book has been edited to help it flow better for the reader.

Certain passages from the Z's that are of particular importance are italicized in a larger font so they will stand out. If you, the reader, wish to simply "dip in" to the book, you can skim through and read those passages to get little doses of insight.

Chapter One

CONVERSATION ONE

Topics

- Oneness is the connecting thread linking us all energetically. Will you let it in?
- The journey of being human and soul at the same time
- Illusionary constructs that block our understanding of our multidimensionality
- Lee's journey with the Z's
- Who are the Z's?
- Prayer: connecting to the oneness that you are a part of
- The addiction to war that is woven into humanity
- The lessons and opportunities in self-sabotage
- Channeling your soul opens you to wisdom

CONVERSATION ONE

DIANNA:

Hello, I'm Dianna Edwards, and at the request of the Z's, I'm here today to begin a series of conversations with them on the energetics of the human soul and the power of understanding and working with our multidimensionality. Welcome, Z's.

THE Z'S:

Good, welcome. Welcome, all, to this conversation. And welcome and thank you, Dianna, for being the facilitator or guide for the conversation. To those of you reading this book, the idea behind the facilitation and the conversation that is taking place with Dianna is, she becomes you. She will ask questions that some of you would ask, and this gives you a vibrational reading experience that is unique — different from when we would speak directly to you. Imagine this conversation as a flow and a transmission of its own kind. In a way, the questioner becomes the bridge for you, but you are also energetically and psychically involved in this conversation. You may find that strange, some of you, to understand; others among you are highly aware of how that works. But we will put it this way: whatever time you read this book, even if it is many years after the conversation was first spoken and then written, you are encountering these words live and you are influencing what you take from it. For we will be transmitting frequencies through the conversation that go beyond the words.

Yes, on the one hand, we will be looking at widening your understanding of your world for the benefit of yourself and humanity at this time. And

even though we will be speaking energetically about the multidimensionality of you as humans and you as beings, we want to remind you that it is very important to celebrate the humanity that you are in now.

We do understand that many of you wish it was lighter or brighter, but what we will tell you is, you are here to create that every day. We put that on you not as a burden but as an opportunity. That is the joy of life: being present for life and creating life, love, and a frequency of connection in all areas. So your relationships, the connection you have to the work you do, the connection you have to the land you live in, even your home and the way that you have created that home — all are a reflection of your energetics.

While we will be speaking to you with Dianna about this journey of being both human and soul at the same time, we ask you to maintain an open mind and an open heart, and to not get too caught up in an idea of wishing it were different on Earth today. For

you are going through some tumultuous times in Earth's history that have long been forecast, have long been prophesied. But there is so

much love, light, and joy not only to be found
on the planet right now, but more importantly
than that, to be created by you inside
yourselves and then moved out into the world.

And that is the purpose and nature of these conversations specifically. They will help you to widen your understanding, your experience, and your ability to create in that way. So, without further ado, we will hand it over to Dianna.

DIANNA:

Thank you. In earlier discussions that you and I had, we agreed that it would be important to begin these conversations by speaking about some of the more vital laws of the Universe. And by "vital," I mean the laws that are in play whether a person is aware of them or not. I suggested that we begin with the greatest of these laws, the Law of Oneness. And you gently replied, "From our perspective, it's just oneness." Can we start there?

THE Z'S:

Yes, oneness. And we should preface this conversation first by mentioning that laws of the Universe are relative. Meaning, a human's perception of what is taking place in their reality is informed by their own viewpoint, their own ability to sense, and their life experience — not just in this human life, but any imprints that their soul has brought in from other lifetimes on Earth as human. And indeed, you also bring

in imprints of times when you were not incarnate in the
physical, but you were perhaps in or around the Earth for a
period of time energetically. So, when we speak of the laws
of the Universe, we have to be somewhat careful with that
phrasing for you all because you (as human beings) have
been incorrectly trained to look at things in a very linear,
one-dimensional way. Meaning, on Earth there is a lot of
black/white, right/wrong. There is rarely room for gray or
everything in between. And

the truth is, there is no such thing as one way.
There is simply a perception of one way.

Because of the human training of the black-and-white nature of your reality, many of you have stepped out of multidimensional thinking, sensing, and being. And again, that is
OK. That is where the Earth is right now. And over the next
hundred to three hundred years, humanity's shifts will be
profound in the direction of multidimensionality and oneness. So, to speak to you of oneness, while you can associate
laws with oneness, we would say to you that, in fact, the best
way to approach oneness at this time in Earth's history with
the cultural understanding and perception that you all have,
is to see oneness as "love." Think of someone you have loved
deeply or dearly in your life. Someone with whom, whether
for just a time in your relationship or the whole time of your
relationship, you felt fully free to be you.

You were free to be vulnerable. You were free to feel safe.
You were free to give and receive love fully. That is the highest octave of love. And so often on your planet, it is pinned

onto romantic love as if romantic love is the highest form. And that is nonsense from our perspective. From our perspective, you all have the opportunity to love one another every day. And many of you do. You help a stranger who you see struggling on the road as you walk past them. You (especially those of you who have parented, or if you haven't parented, have had strong connections with younger children) feel that parental loving, connected energy when you see little ones, for you understand that they are unique, bright, soulful beings but that they need a certain level of protection, guidance, and perhaps help while they are still growing.

That energy of love comes through you as a direct response, and you offer it to that child or that stranger or the person in your life who you love. Perhaps it is a parent of yours, perhaps it is a best friend, perhaps it is someone you've just met who made you feel a certain way. And we should not here disregard the love that many of you feel for influences in your life that you have never met. Perhaps it is someone who has written a book that has transformed you, and the energy in that book has caused a shift in your life — you will feel love toward that book or that person. Many of you have this love for artists in your life, musical artists, or those who entertain you in other ways.

Oneness (from our perspective)
is everywhere.
The key is, will you activate it?
Will you let it in?

When you speak of human enlightenment, you could characterize that as a human being who has remembered that love and connection (also known as oneness) are the highest octave, and that everything else need not be held quite so tightly. For example, those who have achieved states of enlightenment that they weren't previously in (this does not always look like they are floating on a cloud, by the way — they might just simply be able to tell you that they have come a long way from where they were ten years ago when it comes to loving humanity or other beings), those are the ones who are able to be in the frequency of love and connection over some of the, we will say, power structures that humanity has been put into.

Now, to elaborate on this a little, even giving you this notion of romantic love as the highest is a power structure. We are not in any way saying that romantic love is not beautiful, wonderful. And for many of you, it is the way that you open your hearts and heal. We are not discrediting it. But if you put all the focus on that, you forget that you, as a human being, can love any other human being at any time. It is not only a choice inside you, but it is a vibrational frequency that needs to be agreed to. This is why when you get around very loving people, you start to feel a bit more loving. And equally, if you get around people who are conflict based — or playing out power games with one another that do not hold love but instead perhaps distress other members of the group — you will feel less loving, many of you. It will be hard for you to feel that frequency, for oneness needs to be a cocreated reality.

So yes, you may access a certain level of oneness inside your-self through a meditation or a practice that you have, or by going into nature. And you might feel at one with nature because you and nature can align in that frequency of one-ness. But

*creating a frequency of oneness
with another human being, which is simply
creating love with another human being,
is incredibly powerful.*

And when you can spread that around and among other humans, it is extraordinary. Sometimes creating that fre-quency will mean taking an action. Perhaps you will be kind in your words or your behaviors toward another, uplifting them through the kindness that you give to them. Other times you may do nothing but simply feel that love in your heart, and they will see it in your eyes. And they equally will respond. And their own ability to love will increase a lit-tle more. So, oneness can be described in a myriad of ways, and we are simply scratching the surface here, but that is enough.

*Truly, oneness is the connective thread
that links all of you energetically.*

And when you realize that all of you are linked energetically, you play separation games far less.

DIANNA:

Thank you for that. I appreciate such a strong opening explanation of oneness, as it's something we need to be anchored in for all the other discussions about soul and humanity and such to make sense, and we will be returning to that topic. But now I want to ask you this: How is it possible that I'm sitting here in a chair on third-dimensional Earth having a conversation with ninth-dimensional beings?

THE Z'S:

Because you are not *just* sitting in a chair on third-dimensional Earth. You are also in the ninth dimension yourself. It is just that the focal point of your awareness is not there most of the time, and nor should it be. We always say that it is a wonderful thing to be human, and we know that that greatly distresses the many of you who are struggling or grappling with your difficulties about the planet at this time. And what we will tell you is, a "dark night of the soul" is meant to be a temporary experience. It is a transformational experience, but some of you can get stuck in that dark night of the soul, and it is difficult for you to overcome.

Or perhaps you have certain chemical or energetic imbalances that need your help. It is not something you just have to suffer with for decades of your life. It is something that you need to give your attention to so that you can come to access more of the higher dimensions that are available to you.

To go back to your original question, Dianna: We will say that at least 80 percent of those who are reading this conversation are what you might call a little more "old school" when it comes to the awareness of the soul. Many of you have been on this journey for a long time, or you have recently popped open in such a powerful way that you now no longer believe that the human Earth experience is the totality of your experience. And there are whole cultures across the planet who understand that unseen worlds are a part of their worlds, woven into their traditions, their history, their education. It is, though, to be pointed out that

much of your connection to other dimensions has been, we will say, scrubbed out of your history.

And it has been replaced with illusionary constructs. For, deep down, every single human being knows they are of spirit and knows they are also a soul. You can only diminish a human's perception of that to a certain degree. Even a person who you perceive might be living in quite an, as some of you would call it, "asleep way" (we would call it a "disconnected way," meaning they have disconnected from all the soul realms around them and the energetics), even *they* cannot fully escape that reality. It is why some of your poor humans get so tormented when they get disconnected. It is why many will act out in very destructive ways toward themselves or others, for they feel they have disconnected from the light of their soul.

And there are many ways your society encourages you to do this. In fact, it is in the training for many of you. And you are here at this very transformational time on Earth when much of that lower-dimensional thinking is being blown up. Now, some of you have long wished that in your lifetime, you would see a utopia happen on Earth. We would ask you not to focus on that because then you are waiting for something to happen outside you, rather than recognizing you are the conduit of it.

So, Dianna, yes, you are sitting in a chair on third-dimensional Earth, but you are no different from many of the other people listening to or reading this conversation in that you are rarely *just* focused on third-dimensional Earth. And you have found a way to live between and within the worlds. You are one who is open to all the worlds of energy that you yourself are a conduit for.

And you have your own specific mastery as to how you weave in those worlds, as do many who are reading this book. Lee, as a third-dimensional human being, has learned (like all of you listening and you, Dianna, over the years) that it is an illusion — or to use an Earth word, "bullshit" — that the human experience is all there is. It is hilarious to us that any human could believe that. And yet we say that not in a mocking way; we say it simply because

the evidence of other dimensions
is all around all of you all the time.

But many people are distracted away from that truth, given emotional reasons to focus on a lesser world, and given emotional containment by the structure of their world. For example, one emotional containment would be the difficulty of, you might call it, making a living on Earth.

Some of you are born into a system or a mindset, an energetic, that makes your life a struggle. You have inherited this idea of your life being a struggle, and you are working through it, perhaps trying to change it for your ancestral line, perhaps trying to change it in the very system that has been designed to keep you in a struggle phase. And

if you are someone working through struggle,
it is hard to be able to access the fact that
there is, we will call it, a magical web around
you that can be tapped into that can both
neutralize and start to dissolve some
of that third-dimensional density.

This is why when people have awakenings and start to wake up to the wider world, they also begin to notice that things in their Earthly life change. They begin to notice that perhaps some difficult relationship in their life is no longer as resonant for them because they can no longer play out those games. Either they see that person less, or perhaps a complete break is made in that relationship.

Lee made contact with us, or, we should say, allowed contact with us, for we had been around him since birth and waiting for him to activate, but we did not fully know which way it would go. We did not fully know which way we could reach him. We reached him first through music and musical composition. That opened his third eye, and at the age of twenty-one, he started to receive music. And then approximately eighteen months later, we made contact through words. So, you are having a ninth-dimensional conversation because Lee is having a ninth-dimensional conversation. And everyone reading this is now having a ninth-dimensional conversation. See how easy it is? And yet the way it is played on Earth is that these dimensions are separate from you.

Sometimes you are told they are superior to you, which is also a complete myth. And that comes from the way that many of the truths of your religion were shielded inside religious constructs that were designed to keep you separate from spirit; to give you an idea that you were less than anything that was found in spirit where religion was concerned. And that was one of the first great acts of "cloaking the truth" of you as spiritual beings. And why is this done? Because all human beings, as we said, remember they are of spirit and remember they are of a soul. So, if you are going to steer them away from that, you had better give them just a few things that match up with what they feel inside themselves. Otherwise, the reality you present them with will feel completely unaligned to them. But if you take a few truths and bury them quite successfully in a great deal of construct, then they will align with the construct because of the truth underneath it.

But you are now living at a time when the truth is rising. So, what we want all of you reading this to do (and this is why your question is so wonderful, Dianna) is to *not* marvel at the fact that any of you are having contact with the ninth dimension. We want all of you to see this as a normal part of where the Earth and humanity are going. And we are not saying everyone is going to be a channeler or everyone is going to be focused on the ninth dimension. But the consciousness is rising on Earth — and others speak of this too, for it is a universal truth. What that means is,

third-dimensional Earth is becoming less and less the normal reality, and the higher dimensions are beginning to permeate.

DIANNA:

What you just said sends me in about three different directions of questions I'm eager to ask. So I'm going to have to discipline myself. And I promise, I will be going back to a lot of these other aspects of your comments in other conversations.

THE Z'S:

But we love your comment! Forgive us for interrupting, but your comment is very valuable and very important, for you are not alone in experiencing conversation with us that way. And we understand.

Remember that as humans with linear minds, even the most multidimensional among you do need a certain level of linearity in order to either open your multidimensionality or understand it.

We do understand that (as Lee would often say about us) asking us a question opens up a whole other can of worms each time. And that is because the Universe is vast. And so, for us to speak to you from a multidimensional standpoint, it will often be the case that one of your questions will open up three or four areas, even though you are only focused on one. We will tell you this: we are very disciplined in our answers by not giving you twelve!

We try and keep it to an expansion of three or four because we do understand it would be of no value to any of you if it was overwhelming. This is why these conversations are multidimensional activators. It is not necessarily that you as human beings need to understand everything we are saying, for understanding is overrated. But understanding is a gateway to opening your energy field, and that is not overrated. Understanding can be the bridge that helps you unlock certain previous understandings that would've kept you away from a greater sensory awareness. So that is why our answers often have multiple aspects to them that are designed to keep reminding you that there is no one answer, there are many. And we assure you, Dianna, that you, like anyone with your level of integrity and passion or commitment to this kind of work, are asking all the questions that you are meant to be asking because you are asking them from the energy field of all listeners and readers, not just yourself.

DIANNA:

Well, thank you for that. And thank you for limiting it to three or four choices and holding off on the twelve because I am trying to keep up with you!

THE Z'S:

Ha!

DIANNA:

And it's a great deal of fun to try to follow the wonderful different directions we could take this conversation in. But I am going to go back, and I just want to check in on a few things. So, you were talking about when you first started communicating with Lee verbally. Lee tells the story that he was on the London Tube when he first heard you. I had wondered whether that was the first time you spoke to him, and you just explained that it wasn't. But why was that the first time he heard you? What was it about that moment on the London Tube?

THE Z'S:

Well, Lee has a memory loss there because we were speaking to him when he was younger, but by around the age of six or seven, it was hard for him to hear us. He was getting more embedded, as many of you do, into human imprints. And at that point he shut down his sensitivity and did not start to reclaim it until he was around sixteen or seventeen. This is quite common for the sensitive among you on Earth. But before he was six, he was in contact with us in a very energetic way, but he did not understand it. And it was very important for him — and we use him as an example because this is similar for many of you — because at around that age, he was beginning to recognize the importance of connection with other people. It doesn't mean he had that conscious thought, but he was at that age where he was just old enough that he was no longer in the stage that babies experience where they do not recognize separation.

Babies feel that they are in the oneness with all the people around them and the world around them. And occasionally they notice they are separate. And that's usually when a baby reacts in a negative way; they don't like it. What babies are often crying about is the brief realization they have that they aren't in oneness. And then it goes away because they go back into the oneness dream. And then they hit another wall where they realize they are on separatist Earth. And of course, oneness can exist on Earth, as we have said, but the way that your human society has been structured (certainly in this past few hundred years) is not to live from a state of oneness. So for Lee, he shut down to being able to hear us and went through a very dark period for that decade or so. Not necessarily because of people around him or anything that happened to him. He was simply traumatized by the world.

And so, he acted upon that in his own ways and had his own destructive behaviors, which he has spoken about, that he started to come out of in his late teens. The first way that he heard us was by connecting to the music that exists on the plane where we are. Now, the music that exists on the plane where we are would be a little jarring to the human ear; it would not have as much melody. It would not have the same rhythm. It would sound a little discordant because music is numerology. So, music exists truly through numbers. You can break all music down to different numerical sequences. And the music that exists on our plane is full of information. It is not necessarily as melodically soothing or as rhythmically, we will say, predictable. It is a little more frenetic and would not sound good to the human ear, but Lee first heard the interface of the musical melodies and our energy at twenty-one.

And then he was ready to hear us at twenty-three. And our biggest issue with him (we always knew) was going to be the shock factor because he was not expecting it or looking for it. And as a fairly driven young man, it was a little bit "left field" for him because this was not in his plan. The reason we share this personal example of Lee is because it is the same for so many of you. And again, part of his shock factor is the same shock factor the rest of you have. You have been told you are separate from spirit for so long and in so many ways that when you first have a metaphysical experience, some of you question it. You think, "Am I making this up? Is this an illusion?" These are all questions you've been *told* to think.

One of the biggest and most profound realizations that any of you will have is that you have always been a part of it. And it is just that you are now remembering it. This is why awakening feels so delicious to people. It is like people wake up from a dream, and they realize that the wider energetics of the Universe that have always been there are something they are suddenly coming back into contact with. And yes, for some of you, it can cause you to reject your human life for a while, but then it all balances. And at a certain point you get to plug that awakening energy into your human self and really start to enlighten your human life, your human patterns, from the inside. And that is profound.

DIANNA:

Thank you for that. I want to take a minute and find out more about who you are. You're ninth-dimensional beings, and I realize we're using words that are very third-dimensional to describe something that is far greater. This often happens with people who have gone through near-death experiences and feel frustrated that they can't capture the beauty and the radiance of what they went through with human words. So, I want to acknowledge that we're doing the best we can to depict what you experience all the time.

According to Lee, you are a group of eighty-eight beings. Now I, with my third-dimensional mind, think, "What does that look like?" And I have to say, to feel safe and get a concept of it, I see you as little orbs of light. Eighty-eight orbs of light. So, when Lee wants to talk with you or you want to talk with him, do you eighty-eight orbs of light all come together? How does it work?

THE Z'S:

Good, very good questions. Firstly, we will give you a human example that will help you contextualize the answer we are about to give. We will use you as an example, Dianna. You are now in your early sixties in numerical age as a human, and you still have the same name that you had when you were a child. And if anyone met you now who had met you as a child, they would see some of the same spark and energy in you that they remember, but they also would be meeting a very different woman. The woman who you are now is very different from the seven-year-old that you were when you were active with soul energy, and your life now is very different from the transformational journeys you went through in your twenties and thirties and how they informed you. And your deep interest in how the human mind works and your understanding of how you as humans experience life in a human body have evolved since those times.

You have changed every decade, and you have become something different. We will say that those who have listened to us through Lee over the past seventeen years have also noticed a shift. And that is for many reasons: partly because Lee has grown, partly because the Earth has changed, and partly because we also get to evolve and grow our relationship.

But we will backtrack a little and speak about when we first came together as a group. We who are the eighty-eight first came together as a group, but as we have said, we extend wider into source; meaning, we are influenced by other people. Imagine you have a group of eighty-eight people who are all best friends, and you regard them as this unified group of beings who have a certain vibration together. Even though they are all very connected, that group of eighty-eight friends is not just that group — they are also each individuals in their own right.

They have all been informed by all their life experiences all along the way. And if they are in relationship to any other people, they are feeding that into the group too. So, when we say we are a group of eighty-eight beings, the tendency in your minds is to think of us as fixed. And what we are trying to remind you all is that none of us are fixed, not you in your Earthly bodies and not us in our "dimensional" bodies. But we did come together as a group in the early 1900s in Earth terms. In the early 1900s, we started to gather as a group, but we were not all there at the time. And one or two chose to incarnate during the 1900s on Earth, in order to then return to our group once out of the body.

Lee did not connect with us until he had come out of his early 1900s incarnation and prepared for his 1976 reincarnation.

At that point it was decided that Lee's design and purpose was to be an orator, a bridge, and a communication connector on Earth. That purpose was given to him because of his spiritual nature and his soul lifetimes as what some would call a seeker. Many different forms it has taken for him — a priest, a wizard (though "wizard" was not the word that was used at the time, it is a word that you use now) — much like many of you reading this. You have had long relationships with spirit in your human incarnations. So, when Lee chose to reincarnate, we started to gather round him as a group and see what was possible, for you must never put pressure on the human who may want to connect in this more formalized, channeling way.

Meaning, this is formalized because it is coming through a language. And not only that, it is not private to Lee. It is something he does as part of his public work. So, there was no pressure on him that this had to be his job if it wasn't going to be quite right for him to be able to reach us, and vice versa, by his early twenties. You see, there are certain parts of your lives that are prophesied, but they are thematic.

They are not detail based. So, for example, if a part of your learning in life is to become a master of the energy of grief, it is not necessarily that the six events that will give you a great understanding about grief are all preplotted and fixed before you incarnate. It is that there will be six events, but everything can be reorganized from day to day as to how to best serve the theme of those events for you and how the detail will show up.

Why we bring you all this context is, some of us have been incarnate as humans; some of us never have, and those are the orbs that you are seeing. Orb forms do not tend to represent humans that have passed over, and certainly not recently. There are some who return to orb form after some decades away from the human Earth plane, but to take the form of what you might understand as "light," which is required for orbs, there is quite a transformation and transmutation of soul energy that needs to take place. So,

we are a group of eighty-eight, yes.
Some of us are deeply connected galactically,
some of us are deeply connected
in the angelic realms, and some of us
are deeply connected in the human.

And then we plug into Lee and his ability to feel, perceive, and use language to act as a bridge for the channel.

Why we bring this up is, often there is the perception that the channeler is some "meat suit" that is simply parrot-fashioning the words, and it never works that way. Any channeled entity you are listening to is always also coming through the vibration, the frequency, and the understanding of the human. Different people on Earth sometimes channel the same entities, the same beings, as other people channel. For example, many on Earth will channel Archangel Gabriel. But if you notice, it is always a bit different for each channeler. There is always a slightly different signature, and that is all well and good. With Lee, the signature that comes through for him is angelic and human. But through us, he gets to connect more galactically. We have to be mindful here because when we use the term "galactic," it may seem very broad to you. But in specific terms, we can say that Sirius is deeply connected in our group. There are many of us who have a deep connection to Sirius. And so that energy comes through strongly in our signature, but we are a blend, and that can be challenging for some people.

We have noticed over the years that some people who like to ask who we are get a little frustrated that they don't get a clear answer. People would much prefer it if we were just one angel or one being, because again, the human mind likes linearity. But we are not here to serve that. We are here to serve your multidimensionality. And so, the way we explain our form to you should not make you fascinated about us. Instead, it should give you a clue as to how the Universe works. We are here in form. We are not always connected to each other. And we, shall we say, gather above Lee's head in a very specific cluster whenever it is time for him to channel us for himself personally, but especially when it is time for us to be speaking to a group of you on Earth when he is channeling publicly.

Do we each have other roles? Yes. Are any of us working with other beings in channeled form? Yes, but not in this specific group. The grouping is unique to Lee. It is not that certain elements among us do not visit other people or that you cannot, shall we say, connect with our group, as many of you have and do. But the way we gather above Lee's head in a very physical way is unique to him. And then it runs like a current through his system so that, yes, our words can transmit, but more than that, he becomes a conduit of an energy frequency that is an activator for multidimensionality, intuition, and love in the listener or reader.

DIANNA:

Thank you. That makes a lot of sense. So, as I understand it, Lee had an arrangement or contract to meet up with you again in this most recent life, to channel and help people understand the power of the energetics of their multidimensionality and everything you just said. If Lee hadn't been able to keep that contract, if something had happened — because it is a free-will Universe here — was there someone else who could have stepped in? Are arrangements made like that?

THE Z'S:

Yes, but it would've taken a different form. It would not have been this grouping because what you are experiencing in this group of eighty-eight are many of Lee's personal guides, although they do not necessarily speak. That may sound strange to you, for you think you are speaking to them right now.

All of you on the planet have guides that are nonverbal. And in fact, you have far more of those than you have verbal guides. Many of you are surrounded by elementals (and we use "elemental" as an umbrella term for energies that exist in nature, in the plant and mineral kingdoms). Many of you are surrounded by angelics, and you may never know their presence. You may never make contact with them. But as we say this to you, just sit for a moment and consider this. Are you aware of beings or angelic frequencies or elementals around you?

There are many of you who are highly tapped into these frequencies. And we will say to all of you: none of you are just you. That might be hard to understand, but none of you are you. Let's say you are reading this, and your name is Michael, and you have an identity, and you are thirty-six and you have a family that you have come from, and you have work that you do. Yes, so you are a conglomerate of all the experiences and the family members that you have had so far. Now it doesn't mean you are your father, but it does mean that the energy of your father and your father's ways caused a chemical reaction in you that you either accepted or rejected (or perhaps a little of both), and it helped you become the human that you are today.

But equally, you are surrounded by beings who are supporting you and — we have to be careful how we say this — watching over you. Why we have to be careful with that phrase is because it can frustrate some of you, as in, "Well, why can't I hear them?" And for others among you, you think this means you don't have to take care of yourself because someone else is going to take care of it for you. This idea that you can pray to some outside force and they will do it all for you is another way that spirituality has been, we will say, bastardized on Earth. And we say, "No" —

you are praying with the force. You are in the force. You are part of it. And praying is just making contact with that which already exists.

It is not writing a begging letter to some superior force outside you. And forgive us for our "insistent energy" here, but we have to address this, for it is one of the ways that many of you have been disenfranchised from your own sense of spirit, this idea that it is some force far away from you that you have to reach across to and connect with. Now, if that notion is bringing you comfort, love in your heart, and a feeling of connection, wonderful. But many people have not reached that yet through these praying methods. They still see spirit as separate from themselves. And that sense of separation is the cause of disease on the planet, physical and emotional and mental. So, the reason we stress this is so that you can get clear about it. You may already be clear about it for yourselves, but others around you may not.

So, to return to this Michael figure: Michael is, let's say, somewhat angelic in nature, and everyone who knows him says, "Michael, you are so loving. You are so kind. You're very angelic, and you're always soft or sensitive." And of course, Michael is a human. So, Michael wonders about what they're saying. He goes, "Well, I have my dark days too. And I have my tough thoughts, and there are times I don't feel so loving or so kind." But that is part of being a multi-dimensional human. You will go through all kinds of aspects, but if a consistent group of people are saying the same things about you, it means that the frequency that they experience you as is consistently angelic, which means you have a lot of angels in your midst. You are tapped into the angelic frequencies.

All on Earth are different, by the way. There are some who come in strongly wired to the angelic realm. There are some who come in strongly wired to the elemental. There are some who come in strongly attached to the element of fire. They are sometimes the antagonists, but they have also been wonderful leaders on your planet. And they have been able to use that fire to change the world. You are all connected to elemental energies in many different ways. And this is how you become who you are and why you are who you are today. So, when we give the example of Lee's guide team, that is what we are referring to. Are they a part of these conversations? Yes. However, I have been the lead spokesperson for Lee ever since we first met, for that is easier for him.

And yes, he knows that I am not a singular voice. Early in our communication, Lee asked me for my name. And the name for myself that I gave to him (because it is the closest name I can give him to my actual name) is human in form. Earlier I mentioned the music from my plane of existence, which does not sound harmonic like human ears would hear harmonic music on the planet. It's a different kind of music. And similarly, our language and our names are a little different also. But

Zachary is the name that I gave myself when Lee asked. I am the lead spokesperson because part of my skill is being able to interface with language in a way that conveys energy.

I am not standing alone being this hybrid translator for and with Lee for these words. I am, of course, tapped into both Lee and the group of eighty-eight. And then we, as a group of eighty-eight, are wider. And in fact, in the past two or three years, we have been reaching wider and wider. Not necessarily because it is our choice, but because the net of consciousness is getting stronger on Earth, which means you are all beginning to connect a little bit more than ever before.

Which means that we on our dimensional plane are also connecting wider than before in order to strengthen that consciousness shift on the planet. A lot of the work that we do is energetic strengthening, in much the same way that you have people on Earth whose work is tending to the land. Their gift and their skill and their joy are in helping the land remain robust and strong. Most of us in this group are stabilizing energetics and harmonizing energetics, weaving energy. Some of you might see it as cleaning energy, and that is part of our work.

DIANNA:

I appreciate that answer, and it brought up another question I have, about prayer and how we connect and speak with our guides — our angelic guides, our galactic guides, our elemental guides, and such. I grew up thinking the only way to reach out in prayer was through "higher-ups" in different forms that were on the Earth or in school systems I was attending. And there was this notion, "I hope I'm not bothering them...do they have time? Am I deserving enough?" There's a lot of that kind of energy around prayer or meditation or whatever word we choose to use.

THE Z'S:

Prayer can be a wonderful entry point or gateway for many. The problem is if they don't go beyond it. And if they don't go beyond it, for many it can get confining to their souls. And in fact, it can start to erode their souls if they spend many, many, many, many years thinking that they have to keep praying outside themselves and that they don't have their own inner connection to spirit.

The other point that you've made here is the widespread misconception that you could be bothering angels or energetic beings that you want to contact, or that you are taking up too much of their time. And that is, again, something that all of you are innocent of. It was simply wired into your consciousness. You were trained into that belief.

We will tell you that time does not exist for us the way it does for you. And we have said this several times through Lee

over the years in various recordings, classes, workshops —
you *have* to ask.

If you don't ask, we often don't have
the ability to step in and help.

Take, for example, this conversation. Yes, it was something
that we wanted to do with you, but Lee is always calling us
in, and he has a relationship where he calls upon us. And
Dianna, you and Lee in your friendship over the years have
had many times where you have sat down and called us in
to have a conversation that is just private in nature. So you
are all, you see, collaborating in this. It is not that we just
beamed in and surprised you all today. There is an act of
cocreation and collaboration, and we would like to remind
everyone reading this book that it is part of the deal here.

If you were distressed, a good friend of yours would love to
hear from you and be able to help you; it is the same for us.
However, there is a limit to how much we can actively help
when a human has pulled themselves away, back, or down
from help. If a human is in what you would call a "contracted
state," we can certainly help energetically and do our best to
help lift them or send people, events, phenomena their way
that might help them remember the light. But if the human
is deeply contracted, we have to wait for that contraction to
minimize somewhat before we can get closer. And

prayer is actually a good idea if you
understand that prayer is not an act of praying

to other, but instead connecting
to the oneness that you are also a part of.
And doing that actively.

DIANNA:

Thank you for confirming that we humans have to ask for help from our guides. We can't assume that you — orbs of light or guides or angels — are just going to magically know what we need. We have to ask you because otherwise you're not allowed to step in. Is that correct based on what you just said?

THE Z'S:

It is correct. There are ways that we can and do step in, but there are limits.

We will give you this example: We are not able to step in and stop war on your planet. But if all on Earth were aware of the spiritual nature that they share and the oneness they have come from, there would be no more war. It is the raising of consciousness on Earth that will bring an end to war. The addiction to war that is woven into humanity and the justifications for war that humanity comes up with have to die on Earth. And that addiction is currently going through a very slow death, but a death nonetheless, though it might take many, many, many, many decades.

However, you must not give up hope when you hear us say that. You are here to be part of that change. So, keep working on behalf of the light when you can, rather than becoming obsessed with what the dark might be doing on the planet. For that will be debilitating to most of you.

But to go back to your question, the importance of asking for help is not even about just receiving help from another. It is about remembering you have access to help, and the power to ask for help when required. So — and Lee will not mind us sharing this, for he says this a lot — even he, with what he does every week, has to remember sometimes to reach out to us if he is going through something that he needs help with. He is an example of someone who is living this spiritual awareness 24/7 now for almost twenty-four years in his life and for seventeen years publicly in his work.

And even he (because of not only his training, but also this human culture that he is interacting with every day) has to remember to get help or to access it, or, we will say, to "send up a smoke signal." And that is very important for all of you to understand. You see, when you ask another human being for help and they help you, the end result is love. In the moment, you might be grateful that they're helping you out of this scrape or this bind that you're in. But actually, when the emergency that you are asking for help with is over and they have given you something that has neutralized and widened the energetics, then a profound thing happens for you.

And it may be subtle and unnoticed by many of you. You suddenly remember love. You remember connection. You remember oneness and you feel safe on the planet — just for a moment maybe, or just for a day, or just for a week. But you remember that you are all deeply connected. And so, it is the same with asking us or any of your angelics or guide team for help. And to get practical on this for a moment, you can simply ask for help aloud.

You could simply say, "I am struggling today.
I ask for my guides and my angelic beings
to help me. Please help. I wish to be back
in light, in love, and in openness."

Now, those are just example words. By all means, you can use those words, but you can also create your own frequency words. Sometimes it is as simple as saying those sentences, even if you don't know how the help is going to come. And we know many of you have busy lives and you are perhaps involved with many people. And so perhaps all you have is twenty seconds one day where you can say those words. And this sends a signal that you are open to receive help. And if you are open to receive, you can receive. But if you are not, you can't.

DIANNA:

So, do we have to ask aloud? Can we ask inside our thoughts? Is there a difference?

THE Z'S:

We sometimes forget to break it down in very human terms, so thank you for asking that question. When we said, "ask" or "aloud," what we meant was, inside yourself. We will say this, though: for some of you who find you are struggling to, let's say, manifest or connect or feel like your life is going in a good way, we will tell you specifically that asking out loud, verbally, or in writing is going to be powerful for you because it is going to shift some of your human self. To hear yourself say these things out loud, to allow these words through your body, it causes a shift. To write these words down and then reflect on them by looking back at them, it causes a shift.

And for those of you who are what we might call long-term struggling or suffering, then you need to change some of your patterns. You need to change some of your actual experiences on Earth, as well as to intend and pray for manifestation. So for you, this will be a part of allowing yourself to see, feel, and perceive yourself differently by allowing these words through your body.

Now, some of you will have great emotional reactions when you do this. You may ask the Universe for help. You may ask angelics for help, and it may make you cry. It may make you feel strange. It may make you feel a little light-headed. This is good, by the way. If you notice these kinds of reactions, it means you are detoxing the contracted parts of yourself and allowing parts of yourself to expand. The tears represent remembrance. And so, the more you practice this with your body, the more your body will begin to develop a new, we will call it, energetic muscle memory. You will start to become acclimatized to this way of thinking.

This is why Lee is forever recommending that you write down channeling for yourself, as those of you who have been around Lee for many years know. As he says: Just sit and write. Ask your higher self or your soul what it wants to tell you today.

*You can sit with a piece of paper and write
down, "What does my soul," or, "What does
my higher self," whichever you prefer,
"want to tell me today?"*

And then sit and write the words that come to you. Even if you think you are making it up or it's just your imagination, that's OK. You do not have to be having some blinding-light, "donk on the head" experience from God. You might not perceive it that way even if you were.

Receiving channeled messages is quite normal for those who call themselves "channelers." And the normalcy is the aspect they had to understand and come to accept. So, sit and write these words for yourself: "What does my soul want to tell me today?" or "What does my higher self want to tell me today?" As you write the words that come to you in response, which are loving, supportive, and perhaps surprising to you, emotion happens in the body, and allowing and acknowledging the emotions that come up for you is a part of the process. It is the body recognizing something that it has long been thirsty for or starved of. It may not have known it was starved of this sensation, but it feels so nourished and fed, and perhaps surprised.

This is why we encourage doing channeled writing regularly. Even if you only do it for three minutes a day, it has a profound effect on you. We would advise practicing this act at least three times a week. And the more you practice it, the more you will calibrate to love. You will have created a new energetic muscle memory that includes a loving lightness toward yourself. We hope that answers your question.

DIANNA:

Yes, and we're right back to where we started (which is beautiful and a great place to end this conversation), which is: the more we calibrate ourselves to love, the more we calibrate to oneness.

THE Z'S:

Yes, and

> *calibrating yourself to oneness reconnects you to everything.*

And we will tell you this: at the root of everything in your life — everything that you are working for, trying to overcome, trying to become — it is all about connection. Because to be alive as a human and to be enjoying your life, you feel connected. Now, think about the moments and the times in your life when you feel deep connection. Why is romantic love so heady to you? Because it creates a rush in the body, particularly in those early months, when you are calibrating yourself to another being who is helping you become more of yourself, who is helping you allow love through your system in an all-new way. That is a rush because you are deepening your experience of connection and you are doing it from the heart. So, everything you do in life is seeking or serving connection.

Now you may say, "Well, what about that time I spent sabotaging myself for three years?" Well, you were trying to shed some of the toxic dynamics and relationships that you either had imbibed in this life or came in with as a soul imprint to overcome so that you could then help others through them. And you were desperately trying to connect with the light through repetitively connecting with the dark, until you got to the point when you realized that connecting with the dark over and over and over and over and over and over and over and over and over and over and over and over again hurts. It hurt you. And it put you at great risk, not just to your physical body, but to your soul. If the light goes out in your soul, there is no game left to play. The game is over then for a human being.

Why we are speaking to you about all of this is because connection is your driving force. Even if you think you are doing some very silly things in your life right now, if you really stop and wonder why you are doing them, you might find that what you are trying to connect with is a different way. But the only way you will connect with that different way is by making your repetitive habit so bad and feel so awful to you that the only way to go next is in the completely opposite direction. But in doing it repetitively, you are also trying to shed, clear, and detox energies that have been around you for perhaps many years, and it is now time to be done with them once and for all.

Connection is your driving force. Oneness is
a place where connection always exists.

When you are living in a state of oneness, you can feel your connection to everything. This is why we want to remind all of you that no matter how much you are needed by your family, your children, other loved ones, or some emergency that you have going on in your life right now — and no matter whether you are wanting to give as much energy, time, and connection as possible to a person or a group you are looking after — you wither as a soul if you don't also connect to what is important to you. You connecting to what is uniquely important to you is vital because then your life force grows. And when your life force grows, you have far more life force to give to others.

Even those of you who have a very tough job in your life right now — perhaps you are a caretaker, perhaps you are going through a health crisis with a loved one and it is very difficult on you and your family — it is vital that you take some time that is just for you, even if only for five or ten minutes a day. That means stepping away from all the relationships, all the duties, all the responsibilities, and doing something that lights you up from the inside. Perhaps it might be writing some words like "What does my soul want to tell me today?" and seeing what comes through. Perhaps it might be listening to a song that you love that moves through your body and unlocks emotions and thoughts, and frees you up from the inside. Because remember, music is an alchemical energy that you imbibe. It is no different from homeopathy. Music is an energetic healer, and it moves through your body from head to toe and it unlocks different parts of you. It is very soothing. So, find the music that works for you. Find out if dancing in your living room works for you. Find that friend who you can call for five, ten minutes, who is going to reconnect you to the light.

These are tumultuous times on Earth, yes. But they are tumultuous on the lower dimensions. The higher dimensions are coming in higher than ever. And it is going to be your path to connect with them more than you ever have before. And then, in the case of most of you reading this, you will become a powerful conduit for those energies on Earth. Good.

A pleasure to have this conversation with you, and this is conversation one. Dianna, thank you for calibrating yourself to what was needed and your eloquence and brilliance. And to all of you reading, thank you for the time, energy, and space you have given to us.

Dianna, do you have any final words?

DIANNA:

I just want to thank you for a most interesting and inspiring first conversation, and I'm really looking forward to the next one. So, until next time.

THE Z'S:

Good, us too. Ha! In peace and in love to all.

Chapter Two

CONVERSATION TWO

Topics

- The paradox of time
- Earth's societal reckoning
- Liberation: how awareness shifts form
- The next fifty years for Earth's frequency
- The importance of living from a more multi-dimensional standpoint
- The power of conscious awareness
- Understanding the terms "dimension," "realm," and "plane"
- Why third-dimensional math can't explain other dimensions
- Creating a multidimensional life for yourself is the crucial next step

CONVERSATION TWO

DIANNA:

Welcome back to *Conversations with the Z's*. This is conversation two. Welcome, Z's.

THE Z'S:

Good. Welcome. Conversation two is underway, and we are ready to take the conversation further and in different directions. So, without further ado, we will hand across to you and your questions, Dianna.

DIANNA:

Thank you. I wanted to ask you, just to start, for some clarification. In a previous recording you did, you said you were coming to us from the future. Now, I believe that was specific to that particular recording. But are you coming to us now from the future?

THE Z'S:

Well, in the broadcast you are referring to, we were bringing a message that was timed from 2030 to 2035, specifically because of the frequency of oneness and love we wanted people to be able to access. So, by going ahead a decade or so at the time of that broadcast, it was easier for us to transmit that frequency because it will be stronger at that point in time on Earth.

We are able to move the points of time, but so
are you. We can speak to you all from the past.
We can speak to you all from the future. We
can speak to you all from the present, in much
the same way that we can speak to you all
from a lower vibration or a higher vibration.

We will give you an example. On Earth, you can watch television programs or movies that can put you into lower vibrations — fear — or higher vibrations.

Now, we are aware that sometimes the fear that you can be moving through, through television or film, can be helpful. Sometimes moving through those fears can make you somewhat stronger or give you a way to move it out of your system, but other times the vibrations are low and not helpful. And so that is why many of you, especially the more you awaken, start to be far more selective about what you will or won't watch — or whether you will watch at all. Many wonderful, higher-vibration television shows and movies exist on your planet. So, it is important to understand that anything (including this conversation with us) can move you from one point to another. And the most important thing for you to do is to get adept at noticing — to notice when your energy shifts because of the presence of a person, or your own thoughts, or a place that you have visited — and to be sensitive to and aware of that.

Back to your original question: We are speaking to you today from a multitude of time points, and it depends on the listener or reader. We are somewhat in the present: This is being recorded at the end of the year 2021. And we will tell you that we are speaking to you from the range of time that spans 2021 to 2028, with occasional moments where we are popping into the 2030s. And every now and then in these conversations, we will get into the 2040s. Now, that might seem odd to your mind or like a puzzle you have to solve, but you do not. You are always going in and out of the future in yourselves as human beings. You are sometimes in the past, sometimes in the present, sometimes in the future.

The reason that we speak to you from different positions in time is because it will help you to raise your own frequency and calibrate.

We ourselves are not literally jumping time in order to do that; we are simply directing our focus of conscious attention. We do not necessarily exist in the present moment the way you do in your dimensional bodies, but we exist because we are coming to you through your dimensional bodies. So, you are all having what some of you would refer to right now as a "contact experience."

Many times on Earth, people speak about extraterrestrial activity or contact with extraterrestrials as a contact experience. And while it can play out in the physical that way, we would say that any time that you are interacting with other dimensions on the planet, you are having a contact experience.

DIANNA:

That feels correct, but my brain is having a really hard time understanding how you could be coming to us from so far ahead. Because the human in me wants to go, "Oh, really? 2040? What happened these past twenty years?" Because this is a pretty grisly time here, and for a lot of us it's hard not to want to go down the path of "please predict the future."

THE Z'S:

Yes.

DIANNA:

So, when you say you come from those time periods, I have to fight the urge to ask you what happened on Earth.

THE Z'S:

And you are welcome to fight anything we say, whether it is through urge or through rational mind or through energetic resistance. We are offering what we are offering, knowing that you will all alchemize it how you should. And by the way, sometimes those of you who listen to us or perhaps expose yourself to other vibrational information or spiritual teaching (or whatever you want to call it) think that something is going wrong when you resist what we say. And yet what we would say to you is, you are always where you are meant to be.

Sometimes our words or the words of another being are designed to help you look at your resistance and see if you can experience the resistance enough to allow it to shift. To clarify a little further, when we say we are speaking to you from different times, remember, because we are not anchored in the body right now, we can speak to you from any position in linearity, not because we are doing some jumping dance move that moves us around, but because you (the reader) are also able to access the future and the past; you are just not as practiced at it, and the gravity suit of your humanity does not necessarily allow you to do it. And yet there are millions (and we mean literally millions) on the planet who do this. Some of them do it secretly and understand they are astral traveling, while others do not understand it, but it just happens to them.

There are many who have been trained by the ancestry that they came from — their grandparents, who knew these ways and the fact that, yes, you are here in the present moment, but through multidimensionality and oneness, you are connected to everything.

Now, to come back to your term, "grisly time" on Earth, we understand that there is a certain amount of "grisly" on Earth, but we will tell you this: from our perspective, many of you who are incarnate right now, who are highly aware of some of the grisly aspects on Earth, you forget how advanced the life you are living now is compared to where you were, say, one hundred years ago. For the more centuries we go back in time, the more some of your ancient magic and understanding were more present on Earth. There were periods of Earth's history when the energy fields were more open, before they got shut down again.

So, if we go back one hundred years, we will tell you that there is a great deal of advancement in the way you are living right now that exists concurrently with some of the grisly aspects that you speak of here, Dianna, and that many feel and are aware of. But this is why if you were living from a more multidimensional standpoint more of the time, instead of just tracking the grisly aspects, you would be aware of the totality of the whole. It would make it easier for you to have a wider experience of the world rather than one perhaps simply focused on the contraction.

And what we can tell you, Dianna, is — and we will use you as an example, but understand we are saying this to all the readers — will you be in a good place in twenty years' time? Yes, you will. Now, that may break a spell of some of the narratives playing out on Earth right now. In other words, you might perceive that some of the current negative "agendas" on Earth (those that do not want to serve or uplift humanity) will, twenty years from now, have compressed you as a people. That is the fight you are in right now, and that fight is going to be, on and off, a big part of these next few years, and even much of the next decade. But we tell you this to get you to not focus only on the fight.

The fight has to take place so that resistance is present. For if there was no fight in the energy, there would just be a surrender to a, let's say, darker or more controlled agenda. But that agenda cannot dominate the Earth's frequency field in the way that it wants to. It's trying and it's trying hard, because of the approach to 2024. 2024 is a gateway year, and then 2030 is another gateway year. These are two very big axis points on the Earth, and not just the Earth but universally.

This is why things are heating up in many ways on the planet right now. What you are experiencing as "grisly" are some of the (we will say) alarming aspects of humanity's direction right now. And it is a little troubling to you that others aren't seeing that too.

But in the coming two to three years especially, more people will begin to wake up and question not just reality as a whole but human society and some of the darker aspects of its construction.

Now, as we say, "human society and some
of the darker aspects of its construction,"
it's very easy for some of you to recoil,
or go into fear, or feel doom and gloom, or
notice your energy drop. Notice that if it
happens to you. That is you working out
your own emotional reckoning with the
aspects of life that are challenging right now.
By all means, process those feelings, but work
doubly hard on generating life force, joy,
and a sense of connection in your life.

In conversation one, we spoke to you about the vital importance of connecting to that which makes you feel connected, purposeful, or uplifted. This is a practice. This is not a reward or something you should give yourself once a month. This should be a daily habit for you. Not because you are looking to be, shall we say, soothed, satiated, or rewarded — not at all. You do this because it builds your life force in a way that enables your life force to magnetize connective energies. If you are removed from that which makes you feel connected or purposeful on the Earth, or perhaps consumed by the grislier aspects of the Earth, you are not going to be able to generate frequencies of joy, light, love.

And that's the only reason you are here right now reading this. You are reading this because either it is your way or mission in life or you are just waking up to the fact that this connection is a possibility. And you have started to realize that there are levels of light and love that you can experience that will shift your life. But again, you do not shift only *your* life by adopting these kinds of practices; you generate that shift in your energy field so that others feel it when they are around you. And yes, some may recoil, some may not like to be in the presence of someone whose vibration is of a certain height or a certain light, but then they can move away. And others who enjoy that feeling will move toward you. And then you will attract others who also generate that frequency. It is why those of you who come together in high frequency feel good.

As an example, Dianna, the friendship you, Lee, and your husband Douglas have together helps you to generate and sustain each other's high frequencies. And all the readers can relate to this. They can tell you of the people who keep them sustained. And the more that you connect in this way, and the more that you get to overlap these frequencies, the more these higher vibrations become part of your new energetic muscle memory.

Now, to go back to your question,

all of time is available to all of you all the time.

So, when we say to you that we are speaking to you with a focus of time, it doesn't mean we aren't here in 2021 speaking to you from this point too. But occasionally, like a chef would adjust a recipe, we blend in a little 2030 or a little 2045, not so much because of what is playing out on Earth's history in detail at that point, but more because of what is energetically available on the Earth.

And the reason we do it is because your body and your soul feel it; because if it is coming in ten or fifteen years in a bigger way, it is already here now as a seed of energy. We are only directing your attention to parts of your own body and energy field that already exist. And by being pointed there, you will allow those energies to amplify. Because guess what? How does energy get created on Earth? Through all of you — ha! It is not just that some cosmic ray of frequency lands on the planet. It is that you'll feel it inside you, and you'll become it a little more. And then as a mass group, you generate it. Good.

DIANNA:

Well, I think that's what these conversations are about — as far as my intent and yours as well: keeping that trajectory of joy and positivity and energy that you are sharing with us now going, making it stronger and stronger and moving us toward this greater future. That is definitely a part of our goal. One thing that gets me interested in the dance of time is talking about the word "paradox." A lot of these conversations that we are having are about situations that are paradoxical: How can two things that seem opposite be true at the same time? For example, we could say, "There is no time, but we're talking about time." Things of this nature are very much a part of spiritual conversations and certainly multidimensional conversations. So, I want to put that out there, both because I realize some of these things might sound contradictory to readers and just as a little disclaimer, because it does get confusing.

I'd like to talk more about the paradox of time. So, there is no such thing as time, and yet it's a construct that is very much a part of our Earth, 3D experience. You, as ninth-dimensional beings, are talking about time and being able to go to the future or past. Now, I realize you're talking in a context that relates to us, but when you talk about the future, is there a certain amount of the future that's written already that you have access to seeing, because our energy has somehow created it? Could you get a little bit more specific about what *is* in the future?

THE Z'S:

Yes. And we will tell you that there are different beings and different entities that have different access to time. We can speak from our perspective of what we have access to at this point, and it also relates to who we are a voice for.

First, there is what is possible for Lee as both the receiver and the knower of what we bring to him, but more importantly, we are right now in a direct dialogue with the many thousands of people who will be listening to or reading this conversation in the years to come.

We can bring to you what is allowed that will not interfere with what you are creating, meaning

we can certainly give you pieces and fragments
of information and energy that will help you
lean into your multidimensionality
and expand your consciousness.

But we are not allowed to give pieces that would be too early or jarring or in any way shut down your possibility. But with that said, currently, we can tell you that the next fifty years for Earth is fairly written.

What we mean by that is, energetically there is a path and a trajectory that you are all on that moves far slower on Earth for you than it does for us in our perception. Part of being in our dimension is, it's a little like having a bird's-eye view of everything that's going on. For you who are living through it in the gravity suit — which, by the way, is beautiful, and as we have said, many in our group have been in the gravity suit many times on Earth and had an extraordinary time — it is often only after your physical death that you can realize that. For as you let go of the suffering, the pain, or the contraction that exists on Earth, you are able to recognize how extraordinary the dance of it all was.

The next fifty years is set for Earth in terms of how the frequency will rise. And to some degree, we can speak to you about how systems will change: some will crumble, some will re-form. Now, depending on which prophecy you tap into and when that prophecy was made, you are going to hear very different colorings of what is taking place on Earth right now. For example, someone who made a prophecy about 2012 some thousand years ago was able to read the future at that time in a way that was important not just for them but for the cultures that continued to revere that prophecy a thousand years later.

However, the details, the energies, and some of the form of the prophecy will have changed during that time. For this reason, it is always a dance for us to speak to you about the relationship between how energy will play out in form and how it may play out on energetic levels. When we tell you the next fifty years on Earth are set, we mean they are set in energetic terms.

We can also tell you that this next ten to twenty years are what we would call a "societal reckoning" on Earth, meaning, society as you know it has come to the end of the game that it has been playing.

What we mean by this is, there has been a very hierarchical structure in your societal system on Earth that has been gridlocked for many hundreds of years. Now, you could go further back, thousands of years, to when the seeds for this gridlock were planted, but it is really since the sixteenth and seventeenth centuries that you have been more gridlocked in the, we will say, vibrational reality of your societal structure.

More and more people are beginning to wake up and to see the imbalance in the power structures on Earth, to see that there is very much an "us and them" mentality at work here. And in this structure, a few at the top have all the power. In reality, very few of these figures are public. You may start picturing public figures that you know, but they are not the top; they are more the middle — the servants or the public faces for those at the top.

But what you are seeing is an energetic death of that group, an energetic death that many of them are resisting, fighting. They're struggling to, shall we say, keep themselves alive by using ever more extreme methods of control over the hierarchical system that they have built around humanity. And as this control increases, more and more people in the world (who have never felt the control as quite so tight before) are starting to recognize that their freedom of movement and their freedom of being are restricted, and their hearts and minds are no longer allowed to be as expansive as they used to be even just a decade or two ago.

As more people sniff out that this is what is happening, there is going to be more of a rising in people. And we do not even mean an uprising in terms of activism. Although that will be one of the actions that will play out, it doesn't need to play out in quite that way on the streets. It simply, at this point in these conscious times, needs to play out in the hearts, minds, and awareness of people. Awareness and manifestation have become very strong on the planet (and are set to continue to incredibly increase in the next one to two decades), and all it takes is enough awareness on the planet to shift the direction of the form.

Over the next decade or two, this is going to bring with it a lot of liberation, even in the face of a struggle for freedom, even in the face of a struggle against the constrictive actions that will be taken and are being taken right now that you can see around you. But it will get a little worse in the next year or two, so that more and more people see it. And at that point, it will be when the, if you like, sun comes back to the Earth. The sun (and we do not mean the sun as you know it — we are speaking in energetic terms here) will come and support the shift, not just in consciousness, but in form, system, and structure.

And a lot of the system that you have been in will remain, by the way, for not all of it is bad. A lot of it will remain, but in re-formed ways and in lighter ways. But in the years of 2030 and beyond, at least a third of the way that your system of the world has been governed and run will start to disappear. And *that* is where the conscious rebuilding will take place.

Many of you right now are already building more conscious systems for the future, and you might be doing that in your local community. You may have opened a small store or shop, or you may be selling goods or services to a few local people that are imbued with the energy of oneness, connection, and well-being, rather than imbued with fear, scarcity, competition, judgment — all things that have been cleverly woven into your system to keep you in place.

And there are many of you who are already innovating the ways of the future. You may have big dreams, some of you. You may wish you could bring this vision to tens or hundreds of thousands of people. Well then, believe that dream. Maybe that bigger vision is not going to fully manifest for five or six more years. But trust that your dream is seeding the future.

None of you are here to save the world. That is an old belief, an old myth, and it is a weight that many sensitives, healers, and empaths put on their own shoulders, mistakenly, because they haven't yet let go of the trauma they experienced through the times that they couldn't save themselves or others. But you can let go of that and realize that this world does not need saving — no! You incarnated into a complex world with a very complex set of energies at work. And war is a huge part of this Earth you are on. We say this not to scare you, but to bring a reality to you. And war does not come from the hearts of you as humans; it has been sewn into your systems, and you are all ricocheting off the energy of war. War is not in your hearts. War is something that you have been taught to play out on both a small scale and a large scale.

And it is *that* energy that over the next fifty years is designed to leave your planet. And

*some of you are now moaning and groaning,
wishing you could see the end of war*

before you die. But that's not relevant,
because you can see it after you have died,
so don't worry about that.

We're seeing it all now from our vantage point, and we have not been incarnate for quite some time. You must also understand that you are moving very fast as a world, and many of you are annoyed that it's not faster. We have said this many times before. If this shift was happening faster on the Earth right now, it could be quite destructive. It could blow up the system before the replacements were ready. Life is driving everything you're seeing on your planet, including some of the more deathly — or to use your word, Dianna, for it's appropriate, "grisly" — aspects of the system. Life is driving, and transition wants to happen.

Over this next fifty years, the departure of war and the entrance of oneness on your planet is going to mark an enormous part of the arc of your growth as humans. But do not be deceived. That will be a big shock. When you have a group of beings who, for hundreds and hundreds of years, have been sewn into this way of being, for it to leave in less than a century is quite a dramatic shift. So, it is good that the dramatic shifts happen in stages and at certain points of time.

We understand that this answer was long and detailed, and perhaps for some of you it opens up more questions, but never mind about worrying about new questions that we have opened up. Instead, sit with the things that we have said; let them filter into you. And they will lead you to your own energetic understanding not just of time but of why this is all playing out in the way that it is and why it needs to take time.

DIANNA:

Well said. And I think we can just take a breath here for a minute and shift back from that very large picture into the smaller picture that comes from our discussion about how awareness shifts form.

I'm a big believer that conscious awareness is the way for us to upgrade our belief systems, disempower the introjected voices that guide us in ways that don't serve us, and bring greater consciousness to many other areas of our lives. To that end, having a clear understanding of some key terms would be helpful. I'd like to start by understanding the terms "dimension," "realm," and "plane," because you use them a lot and we can get confused. I may think I know what one word means, but somebody else may understand it to mean something different.

If we could take a moment, would you explain, when you say the word "dimension," are there just twelve? Could you expand on our understanding of that term?

THE Z'S:

Yes, but we also have to remind you that we did not create these terms — you did, on Earth. So, when we use this language with you, we are trying to help you expand your language understanding so that you can expand out of what we described in conversation one as the one-dimensional way of thinking that you are all encouraged to have. Black or white, right or wrong. It does not work that way in multi-dimensionality, as we have said many times. So many things can be possible all at once, just as you can connect with many different time zones at once, as many of you can attest. But

> *we are going to give you a different way of looking at the terms "realm," "plane," and "dimension."*

Ours is not necessarily the dictionary definition, for there is no one person or entity that can give you the "final" definition. The definition will keep evolving as you evolve.

And these are words that need understanding, so we will do our best to give you a useful way of looking at it. Now, as you have mentioned, we exist dominantly in the ninth dimension, but we also extend into the twelfth and we can meet you anywhere from the fourth to the ninth, depending on the conversation and what is needed. But our dominant frequency is the ninth dimension.

Now, why we bring this up... We would like you to see dimensions not as horizontal lines going up to the sky. Rather, we would like you to think of planes of existence as horizontal lines. So, when we speak to you about our "realm," we are basically saying the realm of being out of the body, the realm of being connected to the astral plane, the realm of being energy beings who have been in form but are now back in the realm of energy. Now, this is tricky because at the moment, we are in form — ha! We are speaking to you and coming to you through the form of Lee. And that is a multidimensional act on his part, and our part, and your part as the reader. We are all cocreating this together.

We would like you to see dimensions as vertical lines. So if the planes of existence we are speaking of are horizontal, when you see things from a higher plane, you are going above your-self, coming toward our realm, and getting a bird's-eye view of the whole picture. This helps you see things more clearly than when you are in it, looking out at the world, seeing only what you are focused on in that moment. And we want you to see dimensions as vertical because it will help your understand-ing of both multidimensionality and connectivity.

Now, apologies for the technical wording here, but this is the best way we can describe it: We are in the ninth dimension, but we are not above you, we are alongside you. Sit with that for a second. We are alongside you. So, to your right or left shoulder, there exists the third dimension, even the second dimension; there also exist the seventh, eighth, and ninth dimensions. You can walk into any of those dimensions on Earth and have them be a part of your human, physical ex-perience. This is why we do not want you to think of other dimensions as "higher."

One could argue that the plane that we exist on is above human reality, human gravity. And yes, to some degree it is. But if we can land in Lee's body enough to bring this message through, and you can hear it and understand it and more importantly, feel something in response to it, that means you are feeling the ninth dimension in your body.

So, you can start thinking of dimensions as reality and also as verticals that you are moving through all the time. And of course there's the vertical that runs through the center of your body, your spine, your central nervous system, your energy field, and extends all the way up into the sky as far as you wish to go — to the stars, to the planets, and beyond into the multiverse. Equally, it goes down into the Earth as far as you want it to go. You are living in a vertical that can go as high or as low as you wish it to.

The best way we can deepen your perception of dimensions is this: See the ninth dimension not as higher than you but as alongside you. And also understand that it is not the dimension from which humans have been trained or allowed to see, perceive, and feel. Humans have been asked to go only between the second and third dimensions. And humans have evolved in the past few hundred years too.

There were always higher beings on the planet. There have always been those who can tap into the higher realms, but also what we refer to as the "sideways dimensions."

And some of you might be very confused by our perspective of this because you may have already learned about dimensions of reality that exist above you. But the Earth is changing, and the orientations of dimensions in relation to the Earth are also changing as a result. Those dimensions can now be here on the Earth, and many of you have experienced that if you have been to any of the so-called vortex spots in nature or have walked through energetics on the Earth that feel like you have suddenly gone into another dimension. It's important for you to understand that a dimension of reality can exist alongside you and inside you at any time. But when you think of planes of existence, while the astral plane is something that you can connect with as a human being, it is something that you will rarely embody. For a part of being on the astral plane is to be out of the body. But this doesn't mean you can't connect to it or have a connective moment with it.

But at this time in history humans will be able to embody ninth-dimensional energy far faster than they will ever embody the astral plane energy, although there is a potential (certainly in the twenty-second and twenty-third centuries) that those who wish to will be able to be human and be astral at the same time. But whether or not that is desirable remains to be seen. For at that point, what is taking place universally will determine how humanity wants to evolve in the centuries to come.

DIANNA:

So then, are realms inside of dimensions? Because some spiritual books I've seen say, "To return to oneness, you have to go through twelve dimensions, and there are 144 realms within each dimension." And it gets confusing fast.

THE Z'S:

Well, it gets confusing because it's all in the eye of the interpreter. If you had five swimming teachers, you would probably only want one of them, meaning one of them is going to be the right blend for you: the right way of explaining it, the right way of understanding it. So, if a spiritual book ever confuses you, don't bash your head against the wall. We are not speaking only to you here, Dianna, because we recognize that you're asking a very valid question. If you don't understand what the spiritual teacher or book is trying to convey, then it is actually of no value to you.

There are many different ways to describe realms, but we will give it to you in this way: your homes are realms. Think of your house, your home, the room that you live in, or the apartment, or whatever it is — that is your realm. And the reason you know it's your realm is, when people walk into that realm, they will get a feeling of who you are, because of, perhaps, the way you have decorated it, the things you have brought in, and also because it will hold a feeling of you. Because that space that you are living in is imprinted by your energy field, so it becomes your realm. There are realms of existence everywhere. For example, parts of your garden or a park that you visit will have different realms within it, different worlds within worlds. Dimensions and realms are quite different in that way. "Dimension" tends to pertain to a specific frequency where different energies are present.

For example, in the ninth dimension, oneness is a normal energy. In the third dimension, it is not. Now, there is obviously a transitionary period right now where more and more third-dimensional humans are moving to fourth and fifth dimensions, where they are stepping toward oneness. They're becoming more compassionate, more loving in the fourth and fifth dimensions, recognizing how magnetic they become in those dimensions, because they are open to spirit again.

They start to recognize that as they have a thought or a desire or a feeling, it is easy to manifest the form that will support that. But when you reach the ninth dimension, you tend to be a little beyond the form; you have graduated beyond those levels. Realms are, if you like, spaces or bubbles that can exist anywhere. And realms have their own feelings, their own entities. In a way, you could see us as a realm. This group of eighty-eight that we are, we are a certain type of realm. A certain family group is a realm. Realms exist in smaller compartments or areas, clusters of energy fields that can exist within dimensional reality or on the soul planes. But realms, as we have just described them to you, become a lot less boundaried or fixed and a lot more amorphous and permeable when you reach the dimensions and planes that we exist in.

To recap, we are asking you to see the ninth dimension as vertical, and we are telling you that we are also coming to you through the astral planes. Recognize there is a point where those two intersect. Picture a horizontal line and a vertical line, and at the intersection point, that's where you find us. And then we pour ourselves down through the dimension until we reach Lee's body and Lee's communication system and your guiding of these words. For even you who are reading this in 2028 or 2035, many years after this conversation happened — yes, you, right now, in the future — you are influencing what is said in this conversation. And that is how multidimensionality works.

DIANNA:

So, is it fair to say a realm could be a sphere of knowledge within a dimension that we can access if we want?

THE Z'S:

A realm can be many things, including a sphere of knowledge. It can be a sphere of energy; it can be a sphere of emotional energy. There are certain spaces you enter in a home or a building or a place in nature where there is a realm of energy composed of debris left behind. Many of you clear the land, or clear spaces of grief or trauma that has been left behind. Until it is cleared, that kind of lingering energy floats in a bubble, forming a realm. In much the same way that we come together to become a conglomerate of eighty-eight in order to have this kind of conversation, emotional energy or even mental energy or conflict energy can form as a bubble realm in itself. That is why certain realms, if you look at spiritual history, can be spoken of as very difficult or very dark. You can go into a realm of darkness that perhaps has existed in a place or on a land for hundreds of years and now is this cluster of energy that is still waiting to be dispelled, dispersed, or released.

DIANNA:

And I think you're back to what you said a little bit earlier, which is that our conscious awareness, our understanding of oneness is allowing us to facilitate the release of some of these darker spheres.

THE Z'S:

Yes. And we will give you a concrete human example. And while the example we're about to give is not something all of you have been through, it is something all of you understand and recognize. Imagine you are in a very toxic or dysfunctional or somewhat dark relationship. Let's say it's a love relationship and you are with someone who regularly belittles you, publicly shames you, puts you down, makes you think less of yourself.

You are in the kind of relationship where the other person is playing out all their own wounds and is somewhat trying to diminish you rather than support you. It is a power game, and it comes from a deep-seated insecurity and inferiority in the other person. But it may have become so crusted over by their personality, actions, and behaviors. Perhaps they are mirroring what they themselves experienced. They are trying to rid themselves of the toxic energy they imbibed by becoming it and playing it out to someone else, because they don't know how to heal it in themselves.

Imagine you are in that kind of relationship, and you are in it for three or four years, and you get more and more sick as time goes on. And you perhaps have to lose more of your friends because this partner or love doesn't want them in your life, influencing you. And at a certain moment, you wake up. Perhaps it is because you realize something, or a friend says something to you, or you read a book or watch a movie and you see your story played out. And you suddenly have the realization that this relationship has been compressing, minimizing, and belittling your life force and who you are as a soul.

That awareness is the first moment where you leave the relationship. But for some of you, it might take a year or two years or three years to be in a place of readiness, spiritual and mental health, and sufficient energetic support in the world around you to leave the relationship. So you leave that relationship, and then you go through a process of healing, whereby the next relationship you come to might not be the best relationship, but it's certainly an improvement. You have the awareness that you can have better, do better, experience better, usually before you actually do experience it.

There are some cases where someone will bless a person in their life because, "They came in and showed me what I was missing, and I had no idea." But usually, energetically at some level they were ready for that. Earlier, in conversation one, we spoke about people playing out repetitive destructive actions in order to try and rid themselves of those behaviors. So,

often you will manifest these very difficult relationships to try and test yourself to see how much you can shut down on love.

But when the glimmer of awareness that you have manifested this relationship, and that it is eroding not only you but your life, comes to you, you will stop prioritizing this other person's desires, needs, wishes.

You will suddenly remember your own soul,
your own life force. And that awareness
will then lead you to action.

That is a very concrete example of how and why it takes time, once you have had the awareness, for you to undo the conditioning that you have been in. This is why many spiritually aware or awakened people get a little frustrated. They have their epiphany, or they have a few months where everything is extraordinary. Then they don't like it when everything, as some of you would say, "falls to shit" in their life, because the life they were living is no longer congruent with the new vibrational reality that they have birthed in themselves.

It is often a very chaotic process. Not many humans navigate that process with grace because they are blown apart or blown open. But then it settles. And as it settles and you start to develop a new energetic muscle memory around being more awake to oneness, you start to create differently in your life.

All of that is to say, yes, awareness helps you to start creating differently. We have, for many years, used these words:

Awareness is the precursor to change.

This is why Lee (and he learned this himself the hard way), always tells people, "If you find yourself judging yourself, and you notice you are doing it, the human tendency is to then kick yourself harder because you are judging yourself."

And he always says, "No, that's the moment you should celebrate." Because you caught yourself being mean to yourself. And that awareness is the beginning glimmer of light that will lead you toward not being so mean to yourself again in the future.

And maybe you inherited that meanness from other people, or other people were so mean to you that you decided to start being mean to yourself. This is how these infectious "dis-eases" get handed around in humans. Awareness is the precursor to change. So even this conversation — if you think we are speaking a load of gobbledygook, but you are still sitting here reading and something in you feels somewhat open to what we are saying, whether you ever read another thing we say or not, it doesn't matter.

What matters is, something in you is beginning to open and you don't necessarily have to understand it. But if you have the awareness that something in you is beginning to open, we can tell you that positive changes to the form of your life are going to start to move into your life in the weeks, months, and years to come. And that is a good thing. Because multidimensional awareness is a positive first step.

Creating a multidimensional life
for yourself (and that can be both
an example and a benefactor to others)
is the crucial next step. And that is a step
that most of you at this point are taking
great strides forward with.

And in the coming decade, more and more of you are going to create multidimensional lives for yourselves that will not only benefit you, but will benefit all who come into your orbit. They will be reminded of what multidimensionality is when they come into contact with it, which will enable them to create more of it themselves at the right time for them.

DIANNA:

So, you've really spoken about the power of role-modeling. And we will be getting into more of that in future conversations on steps we take and how we take them. But before we shift too far, I want to go back and ask one question that I know a lot of people have, or have been taught or have heard, about dimensions. There's this notion that even-numbered dimensions are a transitory phase, while odd-numbered dimensions are actually where we exist in some type of form. Before we end the conversation on dimensionality for today, is there any truth to that distinction, or is it just a misunderstanding?

THE Z'S:

What we will say is, there is no one truth in your question or mistruth in your question. For there are some who have understood or perceived it that way. So, for those people, that is true. For us, it is a little different, or we should say, it would not behoove us or this conversation to go in that direction, and we will explain why. Less than 20 percent of the readers of this book will find value in that area or find it to be a part of their stage of growth.

We will put it this way to simplify it even further: When you are laughing, you are in one dimension of reality. When you are deeply sad, you are in a different dimension of reality. But those dimensions exist in all of you, every single day. And sometimes you activate them, and sometimes you don't. And some of you go from joyous to sad all in one day because of different events or the time of your life. You are all a world of dimensionality.

When we speak to you of dimensions that exist beyond the ones you are living in now, what we are really speaking to you of is growth potential. As an example, imagine a keen runner who is fourteen years old, and they are frustrated because they can't yet (they think) run at their best. They want to run like the twenty-six-year-olds do. Even if you explain to them that they are one of the best fourteen-year-old runners that exist in their environment, they are desperate to get to the level of the twenty-six-year-old runner. But that twenty-six-year-old will exist in a very different dimension from that of the fourteen-year-old. There are things the twenty-six-year-old will not remember about being fourteen. And the fourteen-year-old has mythical ideas about what it is to be twenty-six that don't actually exist.

Dimensions are something you are all moving through in very subtle ways all the time. The reason you often get fascinated with other dimensions of existence is not about the dimensions themselves but about, yet again, wanting to prove to yourselves that other dimensions exist. And if during this conversation you are feeling a little weird or a little different than when, say, you listen to two people chatting about other things, then you are tapping into the other dimensions in existence in this conversation.

And for some of you — even those who are mathematically minded, for whom the mathematics of it all or the science of it all is very important — it actually won't serve you to fixate on the science or the mathematics. Why? Because your understanding of science and mathematics is probably coming from a third-dimensional standpoint, viewpoint, learning. Everything can be broken down numerically when you go into other dimensions of existence. However, would it help you to understand that now? Would you experience it? No. If we gave you the mathematical formula for love, you'd be looking at some things we'd written down for you on a piece of paper, and it would be this abstract formula. But if we gave you an experience of love, if you felt it inside your body in response to another being, person, activity, thing — that would be your evidence.

That is why, from our perspective, it is not necessary and would not actually serve our conversation to go into extensive detail about those different dimensions you are referring to.

DIANNA:

Thank you for answering that. I know that's a question a lot of people have, so that was very helpful. I'd like to end today by talking about something you and I have touched on before in other conversations, and that is humor and the power of humor. And one of the things I said to you in an earlier conversation, which was that I planned to divulge to the audience that the Z's have a great sense of humor. I will let you reply here because you had a very strong response to me saying that. Because I do experience you as being funny and engaging and light. Could you share what you said about humor to me?

THE Z'S:

Yes. We said we are not actually humorous; we have learned to be humorous. And what we mean by this is, we do appreciate humor on Earth, because it connects people to their hearts and to laughter. Laughter is an extraordinary release. You all get a little obsessed about crying, and there's nothing wrong with that, because that's a beautiful release too, but you forget laughter. And

> *for many of you, laughter can be*
> *five times more powerful*
> *than a release of crying.*

And again, we have to be careful when we make these kinds of statements because people can grip on to them in a very one-dimensional way and say that we said laughter is better than crying. No. The reason we are having to send you in this direction is because the power of laughter has not been understood on Earth to the degree that people now acknowledge the power of crying. People acknowledge the power of crying as a release, and they see it as an emotional catharsis, as a healing.

> *Laughter is incredibly powerful, and it takes*
> *you into higher dimensions; it takes you into*
> *bliss. Bliss exists in the realm of oneness.*

We have learned humor as a way of interacting with all of you. We picked up much of this from Lee, who at a certain time in his life realized that humor generated a very important alchemy. And it is something that he uses not only in his personal life, but in his relationships and his work relationships. Humor can lighten the mood, give breathing space, allow people to relax their shoulders, and help people to open. It is a beautiful ingredient in a delicious recipe of living life from the heart. And humor is very powerful and very needed.

It is not that we do not possess what you would perceive as humor, but for us humor is not so much humor as it is "rhythm." If we were playing the drums, every time we did a drumroll would be us bringing in something humorous. So, we are noticing the rhythm that is required, and at a certain moment, it is helpful to give you a drumroll, a.k.a. humor. And that drumroll does something to your body that moves something through you and allows you to then go into the next verse or the next instrumental or the next lyric and be open to it. So, the humor is something we have calibrated ourselves to from Lee, but also from all of you. Because our job is to (as best we can) continue to offer you ways to open your heart and your understanding.

And you may have noticed, Dianna — for you are in the energy field of this conversation, so you are feeling all the listeners and readers as well — how seriously spirituality is often taken on Earth. And we understand why. We understand that for many people, it has been lost or missing, which has caused great pain and suffering on the planet. So, people come to spirituality very thirstily, very hungrily, desperate to understand it or "get it right." And so, we like to use humor to occasionally disarm the listener or reader from being quite so serious or rigid or tight and remind them that their heart does not want them to be serious, rigid, and tight all the time — that doesn't get you anywhere.

Usually when you are behaving in that tight way, you are in the past. You are in some past wound, some past incident in your body, some past contraction, and you are trying to get back to the light of your soul, as we spoke about in conversation one — the childhood soul spark that you all come in with. And who loves to laugh? Children. Ha! They love to laugh; they do it easily. Babies like to laugh; they like to be in joy. And of course, there are those babies and children who are born into darker or more neglectful circumstances who lose the ability to laugh and don't feel safe enough to laugh very often. But

your laughter is powerful.
Think of your heart as being on fire
in the best kind of way when you laugh.

And recognize that humor is a wonderful stress relief, but it also connects you to bliss, to oneness, and to heart energy. That is why we bring in humor. It is not something we are consciously doing with perhaps a comedian's mind. Comedians on Earth have a wonderful sense of that rhythm and that timing, but the good ones are also highly emotional, empathic beings. For they know how to conduct the audience like they would conduct an orchestra and how to pepper what they are saying with heart releases of humor all along the way. So, for us, the humor is a drumroll, which for you creates a laugh.

DIANNA:

Is there any connection to that and you saying the word "ha"?

THE Z'S:

"Ha" is a little different. "Ha" from us is not actually a full word; it is part of a word. And at this point, it is not the right time for us to extend the word. But "ha" for us is "light language." It is the first part of a word that comes from Sirius, and it is part of the Sirian language. It is useful because it connects you to your heart when you hear us say it or say it yourselves. It may seem strange because you wouldn't necessarily think that your heart has such a brusque sound. The way the human mind has been conditioned, you tend to associate the heart with things like kittens and bunnies and little children and laughing and all the soft things. But actually, the heart is a *powerful* force. It is mighty.

So much of your power exists in your heart chakra, the center of your chest. So, when you hear us say "Ha," or when you yourself say "Ha," imagine yourself doing it from the center of your chest — your heart chakra. And you will notice a shift. The thing is, you'll probably forget to do it — ha! Because so many of you, as we said in the prior conversation, have been trained away from connecting with spirit.

There are practices any of you could do on any given day, and they need not be for hours. We know many of you feel pressure around time, because you are all so exhausted by your human conditioning and the setup of the system that you are all in. It doesn't allow you to rest or integrate very much. It likes to keep you busy, busy, busy, busy, and that's by design. Because if you are kept busy enough, you won't notice certain things. The reason we say to you that these daily practices can be short is because that is the truth.

If you just spent five minutes, three times a day, consciously connecting with yourself, and you did this for three to four weeks, you would feel markedly different.

You would be surprised. Because your body would've started getting used to you giving yourself five minutes, three times a day, to connect with yourself and your soul.

Maybe in the first five minutes you could connect to music that you love, and do it consciously — consciously listening to a piece of music you love with the intent of making yourself feel good. In the second five minutes, you could meditate — your favorite form of meditation. Or simply close your eyes and notice what's flying through your mind, without too much reaction or thought about it — just noticing for five minutes what state you're in. And perhaps for the last five minutes of the day, you could lie on the floor with your favorite crystal on the center of your chest, your heart chakra, or any other part of your body that you like. Just three sets of five conscious minutes a day. Do that for three to four weeks, and you will be amazed at the shift.

DIANNA:

I think that's lovely advice and a lovely note to end this conversation on. Thank you, Z's.

THE Z'S:

Good. Thank you. A pleasure to be with you and your readers. A pleasure to be with all of you. So, in the spirit of oneness, ha!

And in peace and love to all of you.

Chapter Three

CONVERSATION THREE

Topics

- A collective conversation as a gateway
- Painting a picture of soul and spirit
- Our true power is our soul
- What dreams are trying to tell us
- What dreams of fire, flying, and water signify
- A new approach to keeping and working with a dream journal
- Water as representing the depth of the soul, a way to resetting our electrical energy field, and a rebirth opportunity
- Dreams as a means of processing past lives
- Grief as a birthplace
- The soul membrane
- Feeling and seeing through the lens of multi-dimensionality

CONVERSATION THREE

DIANNA:

Welcome back to *Conversations with the Z's*. This is conversation three. Welcome, Z's.

THE Z'S:

Ha! Good to be in your presence once more and in the presence of this collective conversation.

DIANNA:

Would you like me to begin?

THE Z'S:

Good.

DIANNA:

In our previous conversations, you said that the language of the Universe is math, and that "everything can be broken down numerically when you go into other dimensions of existence." You also said it would not serve us to use math to do this for these discussions, because the math we would use is third-dimensional math, and it would not work to explain higher dimensions. And earlier you said that understanding is overrated and that we should instead focus on building a bridge to open the gateway.

So, instead of writing down the mathematical equation to love or to what another dimension is, I suggest we paint a picture and tell some stories that would evoke the "feeling" sense of the energetics of our multidimensional selves.

One reason I think this approach will be more useful is that I am aware we remember things approximately 60 percent better if they're associated with an image. So, let's paint some images as we expand on these topics. Let's imagine in the middle of this room, as you speak, there is a big blank canvas. And floating all around the room are tubes of phenomenally beautiful colors of paint. You say we are of spirit, but we are a soul first. If spirit has a color, and soul has a color, which of these do we apply to our blank canvas first?

Is one the background color that we will paint the rest of the painting on? Could you express this to us in your words?

THE Z'S:

If you were looking at what some of you would call a "still life" painting or a realistic art piece, perhaps an image of a home in the countryside, you could say (and this is just an example, not necessarily 100 percent accurate) that spirit is the countryside in the painting, and the house is the soul. So you see, what we mean when we say understanding is limited or can be overrated is that

the human mind has been trained
to forget multidimensionality, but the soul
never forgets multidimensionality.

The soul is the sensory part of you that is able to feel your way through the world and feel your way through the connections you have to everything.

Now, the way your planet looks now, at the end of the year 2021, when this recording is taking place, is very much what we would call "semi-souled." The reason we describe it this way is because much of your human system comes from a hierarchical and limited understanding. It does not necessarily come from a oneness or collective energy field. That is individually kept right now. Meaning, there are individuals all across your planet (including, we will say, 90-something percent of you reading this) who are tapping into your soul more and imprinting on the planet through your soul. Essentially, you are changing the painting.

If we go back to this house in the countryside, the way we can describe it is this: The countryside in the painting might be the most beautiful thing, for nature is alive. Nature is both soul and spirit, although the soul of nature is different from the soul of humanity. It is more collective and less fixed. The soul inside humanity has been, shall we say, squashed or tamped down, and you all have been taught to separate from each other in ways that not only are unhealthy but give you a great deal of work to do.

Those of you who speak of being in a
healing mode, or actively healing, what you
are actually healing is the wound of humanity.
You are healing the wound of humanity
in order to get back to your soul.

So, we would say that the house in the countryside is the least interesting part of the image, representative of more of your current world. Imagine it is a brick house — brown brick, somewhat nondescript — and doesn't feel great when you look at it. It seems standard, like it's holding up the roof and is a place of shelter for people, but it's not very eminent.

When you gaze upon this painting, you will see this beautiful nature around the house, but the house does not feel as alive or as embodied as the nature does. Now, imagine a week later (and you are the artist of this painting, by the way), you come back to this painting, and you suddenly bring this house to life. Perhaps you even redesign the architecture. You put in more windows. You paint in different colors. You give it interesting features so that now, when you share this painting with other people, what they see is the soul of a house that draws their attention as much as the nature around the house does. No longer is the house this somewhat limited brown concoction in the middle of this sea of soulful nature. Now, the house is eminent. It is an alive, awake soul. This house is now that person at a party who seems to somehow glow, or emanate, or be very present with their heart.

And they stand out from everyone else at the party, but not because they are trying to do anything or get people's attention. That is different; that is people playing hierarchical human attention games, which relates to power imbalance. No, we are speaking about the magnetic soul at the party who you simply can't take your eyes off because your soul is seeing another soul expressing itself beautifully and widely.

This house now has soul, and it lives in the spirit of the land. This is like those of you who get more in touch with your soul as your life goes on. Perhaps you heal some of the human "muck" that you have had to deal with. And when we say this, by the way, we don't mean to paint a very negative picture of humanity, for that can be done by your own people and your own structures. We aren't trying to make you think badly of who you are as humans. We are simply trying to remind you that

as humans, you have been trained to forget
your true power, which is your soul.

And as a soul, when you become more awake to what is inside you that is uniquely yours, what some would refer to as your "soul power" — your powers, your unique gifts, your unique way of seeing the world — and you bring that out into your life, then you get to cocreate with spirit.

To go back to your original question, Dianna: soul and spirit, when they are in harmony, create the most magnificent painting. But too often on your planet, you get one or the other. You are all able to say how beautiful nature is, and you can sense that. And those who have awoken to their soul, they feel nature's beauty even more deeply, because they sense the aliveness in nature that is missing from so many of the concrete buildings that have been constructed for you all.

But equally, this soul that so many of you possess creates spirit. Because

when you are connected to your soul,
you are at one with spiritual energy.

When you are shut down from your soul (or you have re-pressed it successfully, or life circumstances have made you tuck it away for a rainy day because it became problematic to be fully yourself, and other humans taught you this or made you think this), you start to lose your connection to spirit. Because your soul is a sensory being that is highly aware of spirit. There are those on Earth who are that beautiful house in the painting. And through being the animated soul that they are, they infuse spiritual energy into the groups of people around them and into the areas where they live. These are the people who, when you visit their homes, you notice how alive the home feels. It does not feel dead, or trapped, or like it is a pale imitation of everyone else's house. No, you feel the spiritual energy inside the home.

We appreciate your asking for a differentiation. We will say that soul and spirit work in conjunction, but so often, they have been separated. Sometimes, it is bringing your soul online that will help you see, feel, and connect with spirit. Other times, the spiritual energy of nature or the spiritual energy of another person in your life will activate that spirit in you, and then your soul starts to come alive. Spiritual energy magnetizes the soul. And a soul that emanates into a room, into a situation, into a creation, into the world — that soul is able to create, conjure, and activate spiritual energy.

DIANNA:

Thank you for that. What's really interesting to me is that you chose the image of a house for a soul. Because many years ago now, I was studying Jungian psychology, and I was in Jungian analysis for four years. It was so fascinating to me to learn about my dreams, especially the ones of houses. I had these ongoing dreams where I was in a house that was on fire, and I was trying to gather my things and get out. Or I was outside the house, coming back and seeing that the house was on fire and thinking, "Can I get in to get a few of my things?" There were about five variations of this dream. And my wonderful therapist said, "Well, that's your soul. What's going on?" And we took a real journey around healing my soul. Could we have your perspective on that type of work? Because I imagine other people in the audience might have had similar dreams as well.

THE Z'S:

This is the beauty of the therapeutic model. A therapist can (using human terms, understanding, and language) help people uncover the limitations or the wounds they are carrying and allow more of themselves out. The symbolism for you particularly, Dianna (and we will use this because it is a good example for all), was that the houses you were living in at that time, or shall we say,

the life you were living and the identity that
you were in at that time needed to be burned
down so that the fire of your soul
could be allowed out into the world.
And this is true for so many of you.

And again — we have alluded to this in prior conversations with you, Dianna — you are all evolving all the time. That is a given. But there are speeds.

And for the soul that is becoming activated or aware or "coming online" in a big way, that speed starts to increase. For the soul wants to come out into your life more, and you want to feel connected. And you want to feel as if the fire that you are is allowed to burn through your life, warming up your life and yourself and those around you. And the element of fire (in your case, and in the case of all who work with this) is a purifying flame. It is a flame that, yes, can cause what some see as damage or destruction. Fire is life force, and it can purify, and it can transform. So,

> *whenever you are having dreams of fire*
> *or you are aware of fire, ask yourself,*
> *"What is burning inside me that wants to*
> *come out, to come forth, to be unleashed?"*

Some of you reading this are a little weepy right now at this moment, as we are describing this.

> *Those of you who have tears or strong feelings*
> *about what we are saying are the ones who*
> *are here to learn how to let the fire of your soul*
> *burn in the world in a very big way.*

And part of your mission is to demonstrate that to others. All humans are on Earth to see how much soul energy they can bring into, first, their own lives, and then, in turn, the lives of others. But there are many among you whose job it is to be what we would call a "superpower" when it comes to soul energy and the energy of fire. And Dianna, you are one of those, as are many reading this. So for you, the size and the impact of this fire burning through your home, a.k.a. your identity as a human at that time, was a signal to you that there was far more that you were meant to bring to the Earth, to your life, and to the lives of others, and that part of your design (again, as with many reading this) was to be an example and an energetic, we will say, activator for others.

DIANNA:

I will say that once I really started embracing that part of me that you just described, the dreams slowed down, or the fires in the dreams weren't as bad. Or the fire would be down in the basement, and I had more time to get out. Or maybe in the dream, I actually figured out how to put the fire out. So, it was very interesting to watch the evolution of the dreams and what they were trying to tell me.

And now, if it happens, it's a much smaller fire in the house, and I immediately know to identify, "What's going on here? Where have I lost contact with my vital sense of self and soul?"

THE Z'S:

Well, we are very grateful and appreciative that you bring this dream example up, because in your case (and in the cases of, again, many reading this, for you are the perfect ambassador for these conversations because you are including so many in the collective in your questions), dreams are often the first realm, or in some people's cases, the only realm where psychic vision activates. At this time in history, storytelling tends to come visually through television or film. But if you go back in time, it came through tribal storytelling, community storytelling, people reading stories to one another. Your mind's eye and your visionary mind are activated as you imagine yourself in these stories, and many of you have cathartic responses to these stories. These stories mirror aspects of your life. If you are watching a movie where something touches you or makes you emotional, often it is because you have either directly experienced what you are seeing or you simply have an empathic connection to it.

Some of you may be watching something that you have experienced in another lifetime, so you cannot explain why it is moving you so much to watch this person go through this thing in the story that you yourself think you have not gone through. Dreams are the same. The reason we use film and television as an example is that, for many of you, your dreams are using visual storytelling and "feeling" storytelling. For the dreams are visceral, and they feel emotionally very real. And that is why you have a strong response to the dream. Many of you are first reached psychically through your dreams. Your psychic visioning and feeling come online during the dream state, because your human self is (to your perception) asleep.

From our perspective, when you go to sleep,
that's when all the work begins.

Ha! So, those of you who wake up after sleeping and wonder why you feel a little tired, it is because the soul comes online in a very powerful way when you switch off the ability for the human mind to engage with life. So dreams, for many, are their first awareness of what you might call psychic messages, psychic information. But interestingly, still, many people on the planet don't quite see it that way. They write dreams off as fantasy or disconnected from them. Or they say things like, "I had a strange dream where I was running through a field, and I was terrified because I was being chased by somebody." Sometimes, if you reflect on that dream, you will be able to see what it is paralleling in your life. However, other times, dreams are places that can help you heal from things that you are not creating space for in your life.

For example, a dream in which you are running, being chased through a field, and feeling very anxious is a way for you to process or move anxiety or fear that is running through you subconsciously and that you are not even aware of. It needs to move in order for you to have a higher outcome in your life. Otherwise, you might continue to play out that subconscious fear and anxiety as you go about your daily life. And then, through your magnetic energy, you will attract things, experiences, or people that will put you into that anxiety or that fear.

Dreams are not only predictive. They're also great healers that move a lot of energy for you.

And for those of you who are reading this with a slightly new awareness of your dreams, keeping a dream journal can be very helpful. For it allows you to consciously co-create with the dreams you are having and cultivate a deeper awareness about the experience you are having while you are (you think) asleep.

DIANNA:

I'd like to stay with the conversation around dreams a little longer, because I feel really connected to people wondering about some of their other dreams as we're talking about this. Another fairly common type of dream that a lot of people experience is a dream of flying. I had this a lot as a kid but not so much as an adult. I was being chased, like you said, trying to get away from something. And I would be not so much flapping my wings, but kind of moving them in a circle by my sides, and just trying to get higher and higher.

And I would always get just above the trees in this landscape I would be trying to travel through, and I always felt something was just at my feet trying to pull me down. It was an anxiety dream, for sure. I would wake up, my heart would be racing, and I would be very grateful that it hadn't actually happened. Can you talk about flying dreams? Because there are many variations of flying dreams.

THE Z'S:

Well, we will tell you this. And of course, these are our, let's say — "interpretations" is the wrong word — some of our "ways of explaining" what you are asking. There can be many different ways, but we will try and keep it focused on the main areas of the flying dream.

The flying dream, for most, pertains to a free soul, a free spirit. In some cases, when you are flying, you are in the realm of your guides.

You are in the realm of your angelic beings. Dianna, we will zero in on the example of your dream specifically. At that time in your life compared with other times, you were not as focused on how unfortunate you thought it was that you were incarnate on Earth.

So in the dream, when you are being pulled back down and you wake up with anxiety, the anxiety is caused by your horror at being pulled down, held down, when in your dream you were free. Not only did you get to fly above the trees, but your soul got to be free of the human burden, the human patterns, the human issues, the human relationship dynamics. You, like many reading this, Dianna, are a strong "feeler." You are one who "feels" her way around the world, and it has taken you a long time to be able to, we will say, own, acknowledge, and celebrate that about yourself. But it is also a part of you that you had to remain very quiet about. Because (a) no one would've understood it; (b) certain people may have felt threatened by it and attacked or judged you; and (c) some people may have rejected or abandoned you because they thought you were (to use an Earth word) crazy — especially back then. Many readers of this book can relate to this experience.

This dream was symbolic for you,
for it reminded you that there are planes
of existence in which you, your spirit,
and your soul are free.

And again, spirit and soul are interconnected. We will put it this way: Think of diving into a swimming pool and feeling the water on your body as you do. Imagine the soul is your body, and spirit is the water. Or think of going into nature for a walk or a jog or a hike; the soul is your body, and spirit is nature. So, for you, Dianna, the fact that you got *above* the trees signifies that you got closer to your angelic team, you got closer to your guides, but you were not allowed to stay there. And being pulled back down to the ground and the anxiety you felt represented you beginning to get in touch with the thoughts and emotions you needed to get in touch with to address the quarter of you that has struggled with being incarnate on Earth. For it is only a quarter of you that has that reaction.

The other parts of you are quite at peace with where they are and why they are here, and you have become more aligned with that as the years have gone on. But the quarter of you that was not at all thrilled that you were incarnate on this planet with all its, let's say, low vibrations, was very sad to leave that dream. And yet, if you had not felt the anxiety or the sadness that was triggered in you by being shown a higher realm, you would never have become aware of that side of yourself. And awareness of that side of yourself is how you get to create beyond and around it.

If you are unaware that you are unhappy
because you are on Earth, you will magnetize
experiences that you will blame
for why you are unhappy on Earth.

You will magnetize relationships that confirm why you should be unhappy you are on Earth. But as soon as you become aware of that part of yourself and realize that one of your aspects — or, you might say, archetypal energies, what make you the human that you are — has this deep sadness that you are on Earth incarnate in a body, then you reclaim your power. And isn't that funny? For many of you would think it's very inconvenient to realize part of you doesn't want to be here on Earth. Many of you would notice that aversion in yourself and start to have all kinds of reactions: horror, shock, sadness. That is just ricochet reaction, which is quite common for humans. You are often taught to ricochet or bounce off reactions, rather than get to the heart of the matter.

Yet, as soon as you realize and admit to yourself that you're unhappy to be incarnate on Earth, but also recognize that there is so much more to your life than just that part of you, then your soul energy goes to another level. And you are able to reclaim life force for yourself. And you are able to (slowly but surely) use the flame and the fire of healing to transmute that part of you that is unsettled about being on the Earth. And you do that through finding the joys and connection points that make you happy and grateful you are on the Earth. That is the work.

DIANNA:

Thank you. I'm glad you mentioned water in the beginning of our discussion about the flying dreams, because that's another big area in dreamwork. In many dreams, I have been in very dark water, swimming, not sure what was underneath me. Or I was underwater. And only occasionally would I be in crystal-clear water. And I realized water is emotions, unconscious, subconscious — different categories of awareness. Could you speak to dreams about water?

THE Z'S:

Well, firstly, you often forget this as humans, but you are composed of mostly water, and so water to you is the home of spirit. Each element in nature teaches you something. For example, the rocks and the energy of the rocks (for all of you) represent stability and strength. The trees are some of the most psychic nature elements on Earth.

Trees are highly psychic. They have a strong energy field of what you would call psychic information, but they also demonstrate connectivity. For unlike humans, trees do not have singular souls; they have collective souls.

Meaning, the soul energy that you feel from a tree is never singular. You can feel this singularity in a human. Sometimes, unless you have learned to perceive the vastness of a human being, you will see a human as one thing, one identity. Trees are not formed that way, for they are not trained to disconnect from the other trees and plant life in the area that they are in. They are able to connect with one another and communicate with one another deeply.

So, each element in nature is present or potentially present in each of you as humans. Water is life. Water is depth. So, whenever you are in water, you are exploring the depth of your soul. It is interesting that so many of you have fears of drowning, for those fears of drowning are simply fears about the end of your life. Many of you associate water with death, and you panic. You are scared about the idea of drowning. And yet, if you think about the way you entered this world, you were in a form of water in your mother's body before you were born. So, in fact, to us drowning is a beautiful full circle because you return to water, though it might seem horrifying to you humans.

Often, you forget you are water. You tend to see yourselves as Earth beings, but in fact, you are water beings. So, whenever you are dreaming of water, you are most likely in the depth of your soul. We cannot say this as a blanket statement, for it depends on what is going on in each dream and for each individual, but in general, when dreaming of water, you are encountering yourself in the breadth of life force; you have become one with spirit. Unlike flying dreams, where you are above the trees and in the realms of angels and guides, whenever you are in water, you are deeply expanding your soul, your understanding of who you are as a soul.

And because it is a foreign experience for many humans to be immersed in a body of water, for of course there is the threat of losing your life,

it is very important that you understand
that dreaming of water represents
rebirth every time.

For being in water brings a rebirth energy. And as Lee has said many times because he heard this from us first many years ago, water resets your electrical energy as a human being. So, if you are having a tough day or feeling "off," go and shower, or get into a body of water if you can. If your mind is very frenetic, or your thoughts have created feelings of anxiety in your body, submerge your head.

You may be surprised to find that just a few minutes after you let water encounter your body, your electrical energy field will be reset. It will neutralize you. It will bring you back to zero. It will cut the electrical energy that is, shall we say, crackling in your energy field. And it will give you a rebirth opportunity. Water has many different connotations, but these qualities of cleansing and neutralization are the ones we view as most significant when it comes to water dreams.

This is an interesting point that we can share with you. When Lee channels (and this will be the same for any of you who are either channeling or going through powerful energetic work or shifts or healings in your life), he loses water fast. For there is a fire that moves through his body in order for this channel and connection to happen. And by the end of a session, the body has become quite hot. So, he needs to keep water flowing through his body in order to allow our energy to commune with him and join with him, as well as to keep a circuit of energy running through his body. For a great deal of energy — soul, thought, and emotion — runs through him when we are doing this.

He is not mentally conscious of it, for his mental capacity is taken over by us. But the reason we bring this up is because when you are going through a powerful shift in your life, re-membering to give yourself water as often as possible helps you reset and neutralize, and creates a current of energy that moves through the body. You can get very stuck in these emotional waves that you go through in a healing moment, but water is the current that can keep it all moving through you. It is why he and we always say, "If you are going through something big in your life, drink more water as part of your self-care routine." Not because your body needs more water, as the doctor might tell you, but instead because your soul is burning through the water far faster than usual.

DIANNA:

Thank you for explaining that. I think it's important for people to understand the process Lee goes through to bring you all into these conversations, and what he needs for his support. I have one more question around dreams before we move a lit-tle further into the soul discussion. Could we give the readers some advice? If they wake up in the middle of the night or first thing in the morning, and they're waking up from a panic-filled dream of drowning or being in water that's dark and possibly dangerous, or any other panic dream scenario they may have experienced, what can they do? What can they do to start to process and connect with their soul messages around this dream?

THE Z'S:

Well, first of all, in most cases, a few short and simple affir-mations would be helpful, ideally said out loud. But if that is not possible — if you are sharing the bed with someone or you are in the room with someone around whom it does not feel convenient to say them out loud — you can say them inside your mind. For example, you come out of this anxiety-ridden dream, and you are full of anxiety. You can say a few sentences, such as, "I am safe. I am here. I am present in my body. I am here in the present moment, now." That will help you shift into your current timeline.

For in the dream, you visited a different timeline, a different place, a different part of your soul energy.

And now, you are back in the body, and you are a little alarmed that the body feels somewhat altered or discombobulated, and it is strange to you. For in your current reality that you have now woken up into, the dream seems like a myth, or a memory, or something that didn't really exist, but your nervous system tells you a very different story.

Also, and we alluded to this some moments ago, it would be important and good for you to write down what you remember about the dream when you wake. Many of you forget the dreams quite quickly, for as you come back into the realm of the Earth, it becomes almost like the dream didn't happen. It is hard for your human mind to hold on to the dream. This is similar to what happens to Lee when he channels. As we just explained, he is not very aware of all that is moving through him when he is channeling us because his human mind is not allowed to be in charge the way it is when we are not running through his mind and his vocabulary. And afterward, there are certain things he remembers, and there is a lot that he forgets, because he was not able to consciously experience it and because we brought a different realm of energy through his body.

So, he often needs to look back at what we said. And those of you listening to us or to other channels may have noticed that there are things you don't hear the first, second, or third time that you do hear the fourth time. That is because you are listening into a different realm of energy, and it is the same with those of you who dream. This is why we highly recommend keeping a journal, not necessarily as a job or by doing it the way that everyone else tells you to do it. You might simply write down three sentences about what you remember from the dream. You might write down, "I was running. I was scared. I felt anxious when I woke." That is enough. And then at a later point in the day, when you are calm and no longer in that same heightened emotional state, take out the journal or the piece of paper, and reflect on it.

And at that moment, without the emotional reaction running through you, that dream will give your higher mind a clue. You will read, "I was running." You will read, "I was scared." And as you read those sentences, you will likely have a visionary awareness of something in your life that mirrors this. You may suddenly realize that in the job you are in right now, you are running. You are running away from the job. You are running away from the commitment. You are running away from being fully present for it. This is where dreams can be clues for you. But

in the moment that you first wake up,
you are still between the worlds.

So, your analytical or rational mind is
not able to hold a space for the dream to give
you the golden insights that it holds.

When we tell you to write these journal notes, ha! Many of you get a little annoyed about that idea, for it feels like you are being told to do homework by the teacher. This is not homework that anyone else is going to see or grade. These are clues for you. If you want to be in a deeper relationship with your psychic self, with your visionary mind, and to not just dismiss the dream and forget all about it, we suggest that you take a few notes. Then, later that day or that week, you will be able to look at those notes, and from a very different vantage point in your body, you might start to piece together what the clues mean.

Or your imagination, your psychic mind, your visionary self might, as you start to read those sentences, show you pictures of areas in your life that this dream is related to. Dreams help you bring the subconscious into the conscious, and they often do it through very heightened stories, almost psyche-delic levels of heightening. But what they are actually doing is showing you what is deeply buried inside you. So no matter how fantastical the dream is, all it is trying to do is blow up into a very visible and visceral format for you some of the energies and emotions inside you that either want to come out more into your life or need to be released, healed, or acknowledged in order for you to move forward in a more empowered way as a human soul.

DIANNA:

In the realm of dreams, as in all realms, there's no past or future, per se. Could these dreams that we're talking about be processing past lives?

THE Z'S:

They often are. We would say the realm of dreams actually does contain past, present, and future — but a past, present, and future that you put there. Imagine the dream is a big cooking pot. And as you, the chef of this dream (albeit subconsciously), start to throw ingredients into the pot for that night's dream, you may recognize that a few past ingredients are going to be useful. It's going to be good for you to see your childhood home. It's going to be good for you to see the face of your mother when she was thirty years younger, because it will help you to connect to a different time point in your life from which you need to reactivate or reanimate something.

Remember, as you go through your human life,
you are given all kinds of opportunities
along the way, but many of you do not act
on them the first time you are given them.

We will give you a very human example of this. Let's say when you are twelve years old, you are offered a wonderful gift by somebody, but your conditioning and what your parents have told you is you should not accept a gift from someone you do not know very well. So, at the age of twelve, you say, "No." And they try to give you the gift again, and you insist, "No." And this pattern continues in some more sophisticated adult way. You continue to play this out until, at the age of twenty-nine, you have a breakthrough for whatever reason, and you accept this gift. And this gift helps you get in touch with love, helps you get in touch with receiving from somebody. But also, the gift is something that's very important to you. It's a musical instrument, and you are still trying to activate music inside yourself.

Well, what if we told you that this is the same gift that someone tried to give you at the age of twelve, but you said, "No"? And then they tried again at fifteen, and then someone else tried again at nineteen. It's not the same person each time, but the Universe will keep finding different vessels, different ways to bring to you your life themes. And at the right time, you will say, "Yes." And as you say yes to each gift that is given, the gifts build and compound until you become an ambassador of the gift. Dreams have this same function. As you quite rightly pointed out,

dreams sometimes allow you to let go of past-life issues that you need to let go of because you are ready to receive a past-life gift.

At least 80 percent of the time when a past-life gift is reactivated, there is a past-life shadow with that gift. For example, if the gift is music, and you refused it at twelve and finally accept it at twenty-nine, the reason that you could not receive it at twelve is not because you were making a mistake. It is because you were in a family situation that would not have supported you in nurturing and displaying that gift. Perhaps there would have been jealousy around your gift, for you were going to be a music master. And rather than have to go through that, you just kept saying no to the gift. But here we are at twenty-nine, and you receive that musical instrument. And when you receive it, it activates this beautiful prowess you have with music. And that is going to bring more of your soul into the world.

But it is a past-life gift because in that past life you were someone who was only happy in music — music was your only saving grace, the only part of your life where you could feel joy. So, when that musical gift comes in, it is quite normal that you would have something go, we will say, a little wrong in your life. Or something will come up in your life that is a curveball or a challenge. This is why often you get a gift and at the same time, you get something that needs to be cleared, healed, or learned. So, at the age of twenty-nine, you are now ready to have the emotional capacity and the strength required to go through the shadow side of that gift. Meaning, you will be able to handle it when a challenge comes along.

We hope what we are saying makes sense to you. And we say this not to intimidate you. Remember, to heal your shadow is part of your work here. And in fact, healing your shadow is given a bad rap, in much the same way that people misunderstand grief.

Many think grief is a very regressive
or difficult state to be in. In fact, grief is
a birthplace. It just doesn't always look like
that when you are watching someone grieve.

But while someone is going through a large grief experience in their life, they are actually knocking down the building that they were. And in the coming weeks, months, or years, they are going to build a more magnificent building — meaning, themselves.

They may be far from that right now, so when you see someone grieving, it may look like something you'd rather not go through. You don't like the look of the sadness or the pain or the disconnection they are experiencing. But actually what they are doing is rebirthing and transforming. Grief is often accompanied by tears for many. Tears represent water. Again, water represents rebirth. You see the link?

So, the reason we bring this up is not to scare you about activating your gifts but to help you become the most evolved version of your soul. To do that, when you bring in past-lifetime energies or gifts, you also need to clear out the shadow attached to them. In doing this, not only will you be evolving yourself in this lifetime but you will also be cleaning up the ancestral lines of the planet that you were a part of in that past life. And how does this planet become a higher-consciousness place? Well, you have to do a lot of (to use a word you would understand) "cleaning" of the lower energies as you go.

DIANNA:

One last thing on our soul for now. You said we die as a soul if we don't connect to what's important to us — uniquely important to us. Does a soul really die, or does it just pull away from the body?

THE Z'S:

It can be both, and it depends on the circumstance. The soul is a little like the pilot light that you see awaiting to ignite a fire. Those of you who are aware of fires that are gas, you often see this tiny flame whose job it is, when the gas comes in, to ignite all the other flames. But until the gas comes in, the pilot is going to sit there quietly and meekly.

Most humans whose light has gone out, whose soul is not allowed to flourish, always have a pilot light inside them that, at any moment, can start to ignite if the right formula, the right awareness opportunities, the right people, or as we said at the very beginning of this conversation, a very emanating soul comes into their life

who they trust or are fascinated by. And when they gaze upon or interact with this soul, this human, they feel more alive; they feel more in their own soul. They are connecting to that pilot light inside them and allowing it to grow a bit brighter while they focus on or receive the energy of this other human, this expanded soul, this emanating soul.

The other possibility is different. Your soul can be, we will say, snubbed out or stamped out. Soul energy can be completely put into the dark. And this is usually when a human creates a death scenario for themselves. There are many who enter into suicide because they cannot feel enough of the light of their soul. They might be feeling deeply in darkness in the world. And this is happening more on the planet of late. These people feel mired in suffering. They might feel the weight of the world on their shoulders, and the light of their soul is not strong enough for them to think they can continue. But there are also those whose souls leave the body.

And at that point, it is not long before either a physical death manifests for them or they take their own life. It is not common that a human can be alive on the Earth and be completely disconnected from their soul energy. Usually, a human can only stay alive in the body for two to three weeks after the soul has left. You see this in many end-of-life circumstances, such as when people enter comas. You see this also when people do very dark or destructive things.

And these are rare cases — we do not wish to scare you. Sometimes humans can become possessed by others. And when their own soul has been suppressed or overtaken or stamped out of their humanity enough, darker or more destructive energies can play out through the body. Now, we have to be very careful when we speak to you about this, for it can be a little alarming to some of you, and especially if you are new to spirituality or opening up to your soul as an idea. One of your biggest blocks, many of you — and this is, by the way, wired into your thinking — is you start to panic about, "Well, who are the dark energies that I would interact with? What if I get possessed? Or what if I get in touch with a demon?"

In case that is your thought pattern, we will say this: Are you scared every time you go out into the world? The potential you could be hit by a car. The potential that an earthquake could happen on the street that you are walking on. The potential that you could get shot by another human being. Do you think that way? Most of you don't. And yet, when it comes to the realm of the spirit, you have been so programmed into fear by your society that you start to think of all the worst things that could happen, rather than all the good things. So, we have to be careful when we give you the information we just gave you.

But in some cases, it is possible for a human body to be possessed, as you would call it, but not in the way that your movies tell you. Simply, the soul has left the human body to such a degree that another entity or being can move in. But we will tell you that it is very rare that this can happen for more than two to three weeks of Earth time in a human body, before the body will die.

For there is a contract between each human body and soul. And if that contract has been broken or interfered with, the human body's job is to disappear from the Earth, or we will say, no longer be animated by soul.

DIANNA:

I want to clarify something that might be confusing to the readers: the notion that the soul can die. If I understand it correctly, our souls are eternal; they will join us again in the next incarnation we choose. So, when you say it dies, do you mean just that it leaves this life?

THE Z'S:

The soul and the human are in a contract. We will put it this way: The soul of us — we who are being channeled by Lee right now — is partly what you are experiencing when you experience us, but we are coming to you through a very specific form. The soul of us as a group and as the individuals inside that group looks, feels, and sounds very different on the soul realms.

When we speak to you about the soul dying,
we do not mean the soul evaporates for eternity.
We simply mean the soul relationship
that is animating the human dies.

Your soul will show up in each human lifetime in a very specific way. That is why human life is (from our perspective) an extraordinary experience. And that is why we remind you that it is. For you are having a very unique experience of your soul in this one lifetime that you are in.

But does your soul move through many lifetimes, and not just human lifetimes — all kinds of realms, incarnations, and different parts of the Universe? Yes. But do those other lifetimes look the way it looks in form when you are human? No. Human life on Earth is incredibly unique. So, we appreciate you checking with us as to what we mean by the words we are using. The soul does not die, but the form the soul takes while it is inside any of you is what makes you who you are as a human being. And your soul is equally affected by who you are as a human being. It is a contract of life force that plays out when the soul is in the human body. And it is a contract of creation that the soul gets to play out upon the Earth through who you are as a human. But when that soul starts to get dim or threatened, or when it is simply time for the life to end, the soul leaves the body.

It does not die, but from your perspective, it may as well have, because you will never see a soul in that same form again. For example, even if the soul of someone who you knew at the beginning of your life reincarnated into a new person by the end of your life, and you recognized the soul, it would be a little like seeing two different people. That is why reincarnation is tricky for many of you to understand. You tend to attribute all kinds of personality ideas to who the reincarnated soul is. The problem is, the soul puts on a different outfit, so to speak, each time it reincarnates. When it comes to personality, while there are some similarities, the soul's influence on the human is unique in every incarnation. We hope what we have just shared explains a little more. We are happy to elaborate further if you need more clarification.

DIANNA:

I think that's great for now. We're going to be touching on the soul more as we discuss death and dying in later conversations, so I'll save the other questions for then. I want to end on one question that came from something you said in an earlier conversation you and I had: that there is a membrane around the soul that attaches to the human.

THE Z'S:

Yes. We will explain it this way: If the human body is your gravity suit, meaning it is what allows your soul to ground and be on Earth, the "soul membrane" is how we can best describe to you the state that your soul goes into when it is in direct communication with a human body.

For when you are no longer incarnate, your soul still exists, but it is not in such form or identity. It gets returned to the soul planes.

Meaning, you become amorphous once more and you swim with all the other souls, and in many ways, you return to mass consciousness. But "consciousness" is the operative word. We are aware that if we say "mass consciousness," you're likely to think of the mass consciousness of humans, and that is one kind of consciousness. But when we are speaking about the mass consciousness of souls, you may look at it as many fish swimming together in a group in the water.

That is what the soul realm looks like to most souls. In that state, you are not looking to incarnate, and you have returned to the stream of life, of soul information, but also of universal energy, universal life force. Some of you call it "source."

There are many different layers to it. You like to think of it as one place, but it is not one fixed place. There are many different layers that your soul will move through when you first leave the body and when you have not been incarnate for a long time. You are able to take on more amorphous forms. So, some of you go and work with the soul energy of the land. You might be one of many hundreds or thousands of soul energies who are working with cleaning and elevating a certain part of the world, a certain part of the land.

The soul membrane that we describe relates specifically to the membrane that connects you to a human body. In much the same way that we have often said over the years, imagine the human energy field, or auric field, as something that extends a good six to twelve feet all around your body. Now, it can get smaller or bigger, depending on what you're doing, who you're with, where you are.

The soul membrane is actually bigger than your energy field and exists around it.

It's about double in size. And the soul membrane, in a way, is a form of skin that forms around the soul. But there is what you might see as a string going from the soul membrane that connects you back to the astral plane.

The soul membrane is the skin that creates a bubble energy field around who you are as a human. And the string that connects you to the astral plane is how your soul accesses higher-consciousness information and past- and future-lifetime information. For it is free of the gravity suit, and yet it has to be around the gravity suit of the human body, empowering it. But

your soul is far bigger than your humanity.

You may have heard many people say that. Now, hopefully, you understand why. It is literally bigger than your humanity, and it is bigger than your human energy field. The edge of your human energy field is the heart of your soul energy, and the soul membrane exists in a bigger encasing around that.

DIANNA:

Well, I think this has been a wonderful discussion of what a soul is and all sorts of different aspects of working with our soul energy, and so I thank you for today's conversation.

THE Z'S:

We thank you. And we would like to draw your attention (all of you) to something here. There are some of you who are a little, shall we say, "thrown" by the fact that whenever we are asked a question, we seem to (from your perspective) open up anything from four to twelve more areas of conversation. Do understand that we are not trying to serve your linear desires. That is how you've been trained as humans. It is all about serving the linear desire, and that is one-dimensional. Whenever you speak to us about any of these topics, while we can do our best to form a circle around what it is that you are trying to understand, we cannot see one circle as a singular circle in the way that you have been trained to, because that is not the nature of reality from our perspective, and nor, we would wager, should it be yours going forward.

It is important that all of you start
to open back up to multidimensionality,
not just for your own joy or pleasure or
experience, although that will make life
far richer, but because that is the path for
humanity in this next one hundred or so years.

You are becoming more aware and more embodied as multidimensional humans. So, the reason we will give you four to twelve compartments in each answer is because we are helping you begin to see the interconnectedness of everything. And so, if your linear mind starts getting annoyed with you because you are trying to understand logically what we are saying, you are probably listening to the wrong source. If more "Earth thinking" is what you're after, go to a manual. Go to a technical manual on Earth that tells you how to put something together. What we are doing is inviting you into the field of thought and awareness that we exist in. We are offering you a bridge to that field.

For in truth — you won't like us saying this, many of you, but it is the truth — we are keeping our answers as limited as we can. We really need to speak to you about approximately (in Earth terms) thirty to sixty different areas with each answer. But that would be overwhelming, and it would be amorphous to you in a way that would not be useful.

So, understand that if you are noticing you are frustrated because each of our answers opens up more questions for you, try to relax a little around the questions. Enjoy the ride. Start taking in the view of all these new areas we are speaking to you about. It is not your job, or necessary, for you to fully understand everything that we are saying and be able to map it mentally. But it is your job to remember that this is how the soul sees and experiences and perceives. There are so many windows that you can look through as a soul. And our job and the purpose of any conversation that we have with you — whether we are being facilitated through someone like Dianna or whether we are speaking directly to you as a transmission — is to open up that multilayered awareness in you. That is the purpose of these conversations.

Rather than getting frustrated about how multidimensional everything is, why don't you celebrate it, and recognize that the linear way you were trained to think is limited?

And the way that you are now opening your thinking through these conversations is very important for you and has very little to do with us. It's not about trying to understand what we think or what we say. It's about opening to the part of yourself that builds understanding upon understanding upon understanding in a multidimensional way.

Seeing the world through a multidimensional lens, feeling the world through the

multisensory being inside you — that is
the purpose of these conversations.

And if you are just getting irritated or angry that you can't lock it down into one thing, well, welcome to a life of irritation and anger, for that will not go away. We advise you to take in what we are saying with an open mind. We know most of you are, but a few of you have some of your human programming coming up and are getting a little edgy about the fact that you can't seem to quite get to the bottom of this thing called life. Because of course you can't. It is so vast, and you are seeing it from one perspective, and that is the beauty of being human. But as human beings, you have been trained to think you must be missing something, or you must not be getting it right. We invite you to lovingly and peacefully let go of that way of thinking. It will make for a much happier life for you, and it will allow you to move more deeply into the abundance and the magnificence of living as a multidimensional human.

Good, in peace and in love to all.

ACKNOWLEDGMENTS

Thank you, Dianna — not only for your friendship but also your willingness, passion, and skill in guiding these conversations. What a ride!

Thank you, Steven and Douglas, for all the support and love you gave us both while we were making this happen.

Thank you to the wonderful members of my online Portal community, who heard these conversations first; your enthusiasm about the content encouraged and supported this publishing journey in so many ways.

Thank you, Anna Harris and Marti Bradley, for all your early work with the transcriptions and editing; Kristen Cashman, for your editing work to bring the book across the finish line; Trent Barfield and Tracy Cunningham, for the beautiful book cover design and layout; and Jake Baca and Davor

Bozic, for skillfully capturing the audio, which became the words in this book.

Thank you, Marc Allen and Georgia Hughes at New World Library, for being willing to work with us on short notice. And to the brilliant teams at Lee Harris Energy and New World Library, thank you all for your work and skill in bringing this book to life and helping us take it out into the world. It takes a village — or in this case, two villages beautifully working in tandem.

And thank you lastly to the Z's, for insisting that these conversations should become books, and for more than you may ever know or realize...!

Lee Harris
May 2022

ABOUT THE AUTHORS

Lee Harris is a globally acclaimed energy intuitive, channeler, and musician who offers grounded, practical teachings focused on helping conscious, intuitive, and sensitive people heal, thrive, and live a better life. His first channeled book, *Energy Speaks*, became an instant bestseller, and his intuitive messages reach millions each month via his free and highly popular monthly "Energy Update" videos, which can be viewed on his YouTube channel and his website. His monthly members' community, The Portal, offers tools and interactive live teachings to go deeper with his work and connect with a worldwide community. Lee offers over a hundred audio recordings and online courses for navigating a soul-led life with clarity, empowerment, and optimism. He also mentors creatives, healers, and entrepreneurs on how to bring their gifts and talents into the world via his free *Impact the World* podcast. His workshops, held around the globe, are adventures into the deepest aspects of living, loving, and awakening. As a musician and artist himself, Lee believes deeply in the healing power of our creativity, and his acclaimed albums, including *I Am Peace*, *Transmissions*, and *Awaken* (produced by his label, Golden World Music with Davor Bozic), have ranked as high as number one on the iTunes and Amazon New Age charts. Learn more at leeharrisenergy.com

Dianna Edwards is a psychotherapist and author dedicated to helping people discover their own authenticity through conscious awareness. She is passionate about developing and supporting ways that each of us can transform our daily experiences into opportunities for self-knowledge, empowerment, and wisdom. It is her joy to contribute her time and resources to the local communities where she lives. She is the author of the award-winning *Meet Patou* book series, written to support children and adults in understanding and processing some of life's more emotional challenges. The books have been donated to educational and health-focused institutions. To reach a wider audience, the three-book series was recently turned into free online videos on YouTube. Dianna is especially interested in opening up the topic of death and dying into a more conversant subject. Her involvement with Lee Harris in *Conversations with the Z's* arose out of her interest to assist Lee in expanding his incredible body of work as the world becomes more open and curious about the development of its greater potential. For more information about Dianna's work, visit wisdomtranscends.com.